SIXTH EDITION

MOSAIC 1

Reading

TEACHER'S MANUAL WITH TESTS

Brenda Wegmann
Miki Knezevic

Teacher's Manual by
Robyn Brinks Lockwood

Mc Graw Hill

Mosaic 1 Reading, Teacher's Manual with Tests, Sixth Edition

Published by McGraw-Hill ESL/ELT, a business unit of The McGraw-Hill Companies, Inc. 1221 Avenue of the Americas, New York, NY 10020.

Some ancillaries, including electronic and print components, may not be available to customers outside the United States.

This book is printed on acid-free paper.

1 2 3 4 5 6 7 8 9 0 TK/TK 1 0 9 8 7 6 5 4 3 2
ISBN: 978-1-10-792199-3
MHID: 1-25-907064-6

Senior Vice President, Products & Markets: Kurt L. Strand
Vice President, General Manager, Products & Markets: Michael J. Ryan
Vice President, Content Production & Technology Services: Kimberly Meriwether David
Director of Development: Valerie Kelemen
Marketing Manager: Cambridge University Press
Lead Project Manager: Rick Hecker
Senior Buyer: Michael R. McCormick
Designer: Page2, LLC
Cover/Interior Designer: Page2, LLC
Senior Content Licensing Specialist: Keri Johnson
Manager, Digital Production: Janean A. Utley
Compositor: Page2, LLC
Printer: Yurchak

Cover photo: Shutterstock.com

www.mhhe.com

McGraw-Hill ELT

www.elt.mcgraw-hill.com

The McGraw-Hill Companies

Table of Contents

Welcome to the Teacher's Manual

The Teacher's Manual of *Interactions/Mosaic* provides support and flexibility to teachers using the *Interactions/Mosaic* 18-book academic skills series. The Teacher's Manual provides step-by-step guidance for implementing each activity in the Student Book. The Teacher's Manual also provides expansion activities with photocopiable masters of select expansion activities, identification of activities that support a Best Practice, valuable notes on content, answer keys, audioscripts, end-of-chapter tests, and placement tests. Each chapter in the Teacher's Manual begins with an overview of the content, vocabulary, and teaching goals in that chapter. Each chapter in the Student Book begins with an engaging photo and related discussion questions that strengthen the educational experience and connect students to the topic.

- **Procedural Notes**
  The procedural notes are useful for both experienced and new teachers. Experienced teachers can use the bulleted, step-by step procedural notes as a quick guide and refresher before class, while newer or substitute teachers can use the notes as a more extensive guide to assist them in the classroom. The procedural notes guide teachers through each strategy and activity; describe what materials teachers might need for an activity; and help teachers provide context for the activities.
- **Answer Keys**
  Answer keys are provided for all activities that have definite answers. For items that have multiple correct answers, various possible answers are provided. The answer key follows the procedural note for the relevant activity. Answer keys are also provided for the Chapter Tests and the Placement Tests.
- **Expansion Activities**
  A number of expansion activities with procedural notes are included in each chapter. These activities offer teachers creative ideas for reinforcing the chapter content while appealing to different learning styles. Activities include games, conversation practice, presentations, and projects. These expansion activities often allow students to practice integrated language skills, not just the skills that the student book focuses on. Some of the expansion activities include photocopiable black line masters included in the back of the book.
- **Content Notes**
  Where appropriate, content notes are included in the Teacher's Manual. These are notes that might illuminate or enhance a learning point in the activity and might help teachers answer student questions about the content. These notes are provided at the logical point of use, but teachers can decide if and when to use the information in class.
- **Chapter Tests**
  Each chapter includes a chapter test that was designed to test the vocabulary, reading, writing, grammar, and/or listening strategies taught in the chapter, depending on the language skill strand being used. Teachers can simply copy and distribute the tests, then use the answer keys found in the Teacher's Manual. The purpose of the chapter tests is not only to assess students' understanding of material covered in the chapter but also to give students an idea of how they are doing and what they need to work on. Each chapter test has four parts with items totaling 100 points. Item types include multiple choice, fill-in-the blank, and true/false. Audioscripts are provided when used.
- **Black Line Masters (Photocopiable Masters)**
  Each chapter includes a number of expansion activities with black line masters, or master worksheets, that teachers can copy and distribute. These activities and black line masters are

optional. They can help reinforce and expand on chapter material in an engaging way. Activities include games; conversation practice; working with manipulatives such as sentence strips; projects; and presentations. Procedural notes and answer keys (when applicable) are provided in the Teacher's Manual.

- **Placement Tests**
  Each of the four language skill strands has a placement test designed to help assess in which level the student belongs. Each test has been constructed to be given in under an hour. Be sure to go over the directions and answer any questions before the test begins. Students are instructed not to ask questions once the test begins. Following each placement test, you'll find a scoring placement key that suggests the appropriate book to be used based on the number of items answered correctly. Teachers should use judgment in placing students and selecting texts.

The Interactions/Mosaic Program

Interactions/Mosaic is a fully-integrated, 18-book academic skills series. Language proficiencies are articulated from the beginning through advance levels <u>within</u> each of the four language skill strands. Chapter themes articulate <u>across</u> the four skill strands to systematically recycle content, vocabulary, and grammar.

- **Reading Strand**
  Reading skills and strategies are strategically presented and practiced through a variety of themes and reading genres in the five Reading books. Pre-reading, reading, and post-reading activities include strategies and activities that aid comprehension, build vocabulary, and prepare students for academic success. Each chapter includes at least two readings that center around the same theme, allowing students to deepen their understanding of a topic and command of vocabulary related to that topic. Readings include magazine articles, textbook passages, essays, letters, and website articles. They explore, and guide the student to explore, stimulating topics. Vocabulary is presented before each reading and is built on throughout the chapter. High-frequency words and words from the Academic Word List are focused on and pointed out with asterisks (*) in each chapter's Self-Assessment Log.

- **Listening/Speaking Strand**
  A variety of listening input, including lectures, academic discussions, and conversations help students explore stimulating topics in the five Listening/Speaking books. Activities associated with the listening input, such as pre-listening tasks, systematically guide students through strategies and critical thinking skills that help prepare them for academic achievement. In the Interactions books, the activities are coupled with instructional photos featuring a cast of engaging, multi-ethnic students participating in North American college life. Across the strand, lectures and dialogues are broken down into manageable parts giving students an opportunity to predict, identify main ideas, and effectively manage lengthy input. Questions, guided discussion activities, and structured pair and group work stimulate interest and interaction among students, often culminating in organizing their information and ideas in a graphic organizer, writing, and/or making a presentation to the class. Pronunciation is highlighted in every chapter, an aid to improving both listening comprehension and speaking fluency. Enhanced focus on vocabulary building is developed throughout and a list of target words for each chapter is provided so students can interact meaningfully with the material. Finally, Online Learning Center features MP3 files from the Student Book audio program for students to download onto portable digital audio players.

- **Writing Strand**
  Activities in each of the four Writing books are systematically structured to culminate in a *Writing Product* task. Activities build on key elements of writing from sentence development to writing single paragraphs, articles, narratives, and essays of multiple lengths and genres. Connections between writing and grammar tie the writing skill in focus with the grammar structures needed to develop each writing skill. Academic themes, activities, writing topics, vocabulary development, and critical thinking strategies prepare students for university life. Instructional photos are used to strengthen engagement and the educational experience. Explicit pre-writing questions and discussions activate prior knowledge, help organize ideas and information, and create a foundation for the writing product. Each chapter includes a self-evaluation rubric which supports the learner as he or she builds confidence and autonomy in academic writing. Finally, the Writing Articulation Chart helps teachers see the progression of writing strategies both in terms of mechanics and writing genres.

- **Grammar Strand**
  Questions and topical quotes in the four Grammar books, coupled with instructional photos stimulate interest, activate prior knowledge, and launch the topic of each chapter. Engaging academic topics provide context for the grammar and stimulate interest in content as well as grammar. A variety of activity types, including individual, pair, and group work, allow students to build grammar skills and use the grammar they are learning in activities that cultivate critical thinking skills. Students can refer to grammar charts to review or learn the form and function of each grammar point. These charts are numbered sequentially, formatted consistently, and indexed systematically, providing lifelong reference value for students.

- **Focus on Testing for the TOEFL® iBT**
  The TOEFL® iBT *Focus on Testing* sections prepare students for success on the TOEFL® iBT by presenting and practicing specific strategies for each language skill area. The Focus on Testing sections are introduced in Interactions 1 and are included in all subsequent levels of the Reading, Listening/Speaking, and Writing strands. These strategies focus on what The Educational Testing Service (ETS) has identified as the target skills in each language skill area. For example, "reading for basic comprehension" (identifying the main idea, understanding pronoun reference) is a target reading skill and is presented and practiced in one or more *Focus on Testing* sections. In addition, this and other target skills are presented and practiced in chapter components outside the *Focus on Testing* sections and have special relevance to the TOEFL® iBT. For example, note-taking is an important testtaking strategy, particularly in the listening section of the TOEFL® iBT, and is included in activities within each of the Listening/Speaking books. All but two of the *Interactions/Mosaic* titles have a *Focus on Testing* section. Although *Interactions Access Reading* and *Interaction Access Listening/ Speaking* don't include these sections because of their level, they do present and develop skills that will prepare students for the TOEFL® iBT.

- **Best Practices**
  In each chapter of this Teacher's Manual, you'll find Best Practices boxes that highlight a particular activity and show how this activity is tied to a particular Best Practice. The team of writers, editors, and teacher consultants has identified the following six interconnected Best Practices.

* TOEFL® is a registered trademark of Educational Testing Services (ETS). This product is not endorsed or approved by ETS.

Interactions/Mosaic Best Practices

Best Practices

Each chapter identifies at least six different activities that support six Best Practices, principles that contribute to excellent language teaching and learning. Identifying Best Practices helps teachers to see, and make explicit for students, how a particular activity will aid the learning process.

Making Use of Academic Content

Materials and tasks based on academic content and experiences give learning real purpose. Students explore real world issues, discuss academic topics, and study content-based and thematic materials.

Organizing Information

Students learn to organize thoughts and notes through a variety of graphic organizers that accommodate diverse learning and thinking styles.

Scaffolding Instruction

A scaffold is a physical structure that facilitates construction of a building. Similarly, scaffolding instruction is a tool used to facilitate language learning in the form of predictable and flexible tasks. Some examples include oral or written modeling by the teacher or students, placing information in a larger framework, and reinterpretation.

Activating Prior Knowledge

Students can better understand new spoken or written material when they connect to the content. Activating prior knowledge allows students to tap into what they already know, building on this knowledge, and stirring a curiosity for more knowledge.

Interacting with Others

Activities that promote human interaction in pair work, small group work, and whole class activities present opportunities for real world contact and real world use of language.

Critical Thinking

Strategies for critical thinking are taught explicitly. Students learn tools that promote critical thinking skills crucial to success in the academic world.

CHAPTER 1

New Challenges

In this
CHAPTER

Students first read about the world's megacities and the impact of urbanization today. They will discuss traveling to and living in different environments. The second reading focuses on the impact of climate change on travel to different parts of the world. Activities include those to encourage confidence in reading without knowing every word, and finding word meaning in contexts and word parts. Students will learn common phrases and idioms to aid comprehension.

"We don't remain good if we don't always strive to become better."

Gottfried Keller
Swiss writer

Chapter Opener

- Ask students to look at the photo of Seoul, Korea, and describe what they see.
- Encourage a discussion of other large cities and megacities students may know. (megacity = population of more than 25 million)
- Have students work in groups to answer the questions in the **Connecting to the Topic** box.

Chapter Overview

Reading Selections

Overpopulation Fuels Megacities, for Better or Worse by Miki Knezevic

Go with the Floe: Adventure Travel's Love-Hate Relationship with Climate Change by Sean Gregory

Reading Skills and Strategies

Reading without knowing every word

Recalling information

Finding the main idea of a reading

Checking reading comprehension for correct facts from a reading

Critical-Thinking Skills

Interpreting cultural differences concerning meeting and greeting

Analyzing the title of a reading

Synthesizing group discussion and reporting on it

Synthesizing Internet content: Taking notes and presenting results

Writing Tip: Using details to support your ideas

Vocabulary Building

Understanding the meaning of words from context

Understanding compound words (with and without hyphenation)

Analyzing words with prefixes and suffixes

Building new words with suffixes and prefixes

Identifying common phrases and idioms and their meanings

Focusing on words from the Academic Word List

Focus on Testing TOEFL® iBT

Analyzing points of contrast on tests

(Reading: *Two Different Styles of Democracy: A Personal Viewpoint*)

Vocabulary

Nouns
- access*
- channel*
- cooperation*
- countryside
- drought
- engineer
- expertise*
- founder*
- impact*
- infrastructure*
- landscape
- mechanization
- megacities
- migration
- overpopulation
- resources*
- routes*
- slums
- top of the world
- urbanization

Verbs
- abandon*
- adapting*
- emerging*
- evidenced*
- improve
- migrate
- promote*
- reveal*
- sustain*
- take off

Adjectives
- agricultural
- defensive
- estimated*
- finite*
- industrial
- overcrowded
- traditional*

Adverb
- in no way

Expressions
- has lost count of
- lead to a boom
- (to be) rooting for

*These words are from the Academic Word List. For more information on this list, see www.victoria.ac.nz/lals/resources/academicwordlist/

Overpopulation Fuels Megacities, for Better or Worse

Before You Read

Strategy

Reading Without Knowing Every Word

- Read the information in the Strategy box and explain as needed.
- Have students refer to the reading on pages 5–6. Tell them to look over the title and headings, and call out words that are new to them. Write the new words on the board.
- Instruct students to read the article quickly and to skip words they don't know. They should keep on reading to the end of the article and then go back and read a second time.
- Remind them that it is not necessary to know every word to understand the article. Ask volunteers for the gist of the article.

1 Reading Without Knowing Every Word

Best Practice

Making Use of Academic Content
This activity will help students read and understand without knowing every word. By skimming the article for headings and main ideas, and skipping over unknown words, students will increase their reading fluency and be prepared to handle the types of readings they will encounter in academic textbooks.

- Have students read the directions.
- Assign partners or have them work independently to answer the questions. (Answers will vary.)
- In item 2, note that *fuel* is used as a verb. Remind students that it is OK if they don't know the answers at this time. After they study the reading and do the activities, they will gain more knowledge of the content.
- Call on students to share their answers with the class.

Read

- Read the Introduction aloud. Do not answer the questions, but tell students to keep these questions in mind as they read the article.
- Have students read the passage silently within a time limit (10 minutes) or read along as you play the audio.
- Tell students to underline any words or phrases that are new or that they don't understand.
- Remind them not to use a dictionary during this part of the lesson.
- Tell students to complete Activity 2 Recalling Information, when they finish the passage.
- After the class has finished the reading, go back to the questions from the Introduction and solicit student answers.

After You Read

2 Recalling Information

- Read the first statement. Ask a student to explain why the answer is false. (more people are being born now than in the past)
- Continue with the rest of the statements. Make corrections when necessary.
- For false answers, ask volunteers to write the correct statements on the board.

ANSWER KEY

1. False; There are more people being born now than in the past. **2.** False; In 1950, there were only two megacities, but now there are over 25, almost all of them in Africa, Latin America, and Asia. **3.** True **4.** True **5.** False; More than half of the Chinese population now lives in the cities. **6.** True **7.** False; In Sub-Saharan Africa today, people are moving to the cities and are not staying in the rural areas and practicing agriculture. **8.** True **9.** True

Strategy

Finding the Main Idea of a Reading

- Read the information in the Strategy box and explain as needed.
- Ask students to give an example of a main idea in the reading. (Cities are growing fast and having problems because of overpopulation.)
- Remind students that subordinate ideas or subtopics are related to only one part of the article; the main idea is related to the entire article.

3 Finding the Main Idea of a Reading

- Read the directions and put students in small groups to complete the activity.
- Have one student from each group present their answers.

ANSWER KEY

1. S (secondary) **2.** NI (not included) **3.** M (main idea) **4.** S (secondary)

Strategy

Understanding the Meaning of Words from Context

- Read the information in the Strategy box and explain as needed.
- Tell students that it is possible to figure out the meaning of a word without using a dictionary and explain that they may remember it better if they figure it out.
- Have students find one word that they underlined in the reading and figure out the meaning from the context.
- Call on a few students to tell which words they chose and their meanings.

4 Understanding the Meaning of Words from Context

- Read the activity instructions and explain as needed.
- Model the activity by doing the first item with the class. Have students find *an estimated* in the reading and look at its context. Then have them read the answer choices for item 1. Ask which of the choices makes sense and why. (A: a calculated; *an estimated* is related to numbers and counting; so is *calculating*)
- Have students complete the activity with a partner
- Discuss the answers as a class. If appropriate, ask students to explain why they chose their answer.

ANSWER KEY

1. A **2.** C **3.** D **4.** C **5.** D **6.** C
7. C **8.** B **9.** D **10.** A

Expansion Activity

- The aim of this Expansion Activity is to give students additional practice with the new vocabulary.
- Tell students they will write a vocabulary quiz for the class.
- Have students choose three words from Activity 4. For each word, ask them to write three sentences using the word in context.
- Remind students to make sure the context adequately conveys the meaning of the word. Circulate to guide students as they write their sentences.
- Have each student write one of their sentences on the board and draw a blank line to show where the vocabulary word should go. If students have access to computers, you may have them do this on the computer and print out their quiz.
- Ask the class to fill in the blanks with the correct vocabulary word based on the context provided in the quiz sentences.

Strategy

Understanding Compound Words

- Read the information in the Strategy box.
- Ask students to give you other compound words they know. Write them on the board and identify the two parts.

5 Understanding Compound Words

- Read the directions.
- Have students complete the activity on their own.
- Review the correct answers with the class.
- Check comprehension by asking students to use the words in new sentences.

ANSWER KEY

1. *ever-growing*: *ever* = always; *growing* = getting bigger; *ever-growing* is a population that is always getting bigger
2. *countryside*: *country* = outside the city; *side* = next to; *countryside* is the place just outside or next to the city
3. *teahouse*: *tea* = hot beverage; *house* = place, small building; *teahouse* is a place to drink tea
4. *railroads*: *rail* = long piece of material, usually metal; *road* = street, passageway; *railroad* is a street made of rails
5. *ever-increasing*: *ever* = always; *increasing* = getting bigger; *ever-increasing* is always getting bigger
6. *one-seventh* = *one out of seven*, the number of people
7. *overcrowded*: *over* = too many, excess; *crowded* = large group of people in one place; *overcrowded* is too many people in one place.
8. *well-designed*: *well* = good; *designed* = planned; *well-designed* cities have a good plan

Best Practice

Cultivating Critical Thinking

In the following Expansion Activity, students use their critical thinking skills by analyzing the patterns of words and applying what they have already learned about compound words.

REPRODUCIBLE

Expansion Activity

- The aim of this activity is to provide additional practice with compound words
- Copy and distribute the Black Line Master "Compound Words" on page BLM1of this Teacher's Manual.
- Read the instructions and explain the example. Model how to create the additional compound words.
- When students complete the worksheet, review the answers and make corrections.
- Begin a list of new words on a chart to keep posted in your classroom and have students add new words to their personal dictionary.

Pronunciation Note

If you have two nouns that form a compound word, usually the first word is stressed. For example: key+board = ˈkeyboard

Strategy

Analyzing Words with Suffixes and Prefixes

- Read the information in the Strategy box.
- Have student volunteers suggest other words that start with one of the prefixes or end with one of the suffixes listed.

6 Building New Words with Suffixes and Prefixes

- Read the directions out loud.
- Have students work with a partner to add the correct suffix or prefix in each item.
- Then have students compare their answers with those of another pair of students.
- Make corrections and answer questions as needed.
- Have students identify the change in the part of speech of the new word.

ANSWER KEY

1. urbanization (verb to noun)
2. traditional (noun to adj)
3. industrial (noun to adj)
4. mechanization (adj to noun)
5. dwellers (verb to noun)
6. unknown (both adj)
7. education (verb to noun)
8. migration (verb to noun)
9. sub-Saharan (phrase to adj)
10. unable (both adj)
11. agricultural (noun to adj)
12. cooperation (verb to noun)

Best Practice

Interacting with Others

In Activities 7 and 8, students interact in pairs to state and share their opinions, and analyze and discuss photos. By participating in pair work, and listening to and expressing opinions, students are able to practice authentic conversation based on the topics presented in the reading.

7 What's Your Opinion?

- Read the directions and put students into pairs.
- Read the three items in the activity and check comprehension.
- Have students take notes as they speak to each other. Tell them that they should be prepared to share their partner's viewpoint with the class.
- Discuss their opinions as a class.

8 Around the Globe

- Have students work with the same partner as for Activity 7, or assign different partners.
- Tell students to look at the photos in sections A and B and read the paragraph headings and photo captions. Ask: *What do you think this reading is about?*
- Have students read aloud with their partner and answer the questions after each section.
- Discuss the answers as a whole class activity.

Content Note

Some typical physical greetings in the U.S. depend on the relationship between the people. Friends will wave or nod their heads if they don't use a verbal "hello." Handshakes are common for people who have never met before, are just acquaintances, or are business colleagues. Many Americans greet family or close friends with hugs and kisses on the cheek. Many visitors to the U.S. are surprised to learn that American use "How are you?" as a greeting. It is a question, but they often do not expect an answer. This greeting may be the same as saying "Good morning."

9 Asking Personal Questions

- Read the directions aloud.
- Clarify that one of the questions in the list may or may not be impolite in certain circumstances.
- Have students work with a partner and then share their findings with the class.
- Ask students to share which questions would be impolite in their culture(s).

ANSWER KEY

1. polite **2.** impolite **3.** polite **4.** impolite **5.** polite **6.** sometimes impolite, depending on person's age: polite for children **7.** polite **8.** impolite

Go with the Floe: Adventure Travel's Love-Hate Relationship with Climate Change

Before You Read

Strategy

Analyzing the Title of a Reading

- Read the first paragraph in the Strategy box.
- Have a volunteer read each of the three points.

1 Analyzing the Title of a Reading

- Read the directions. Assign partners or have students work independently and then share their answers with a partner.
- As a whole class activity, have students share their answers for each item.
- Solicit examples of other homophones students may know: *sun/son, bored/board, tale/tail, brake/break, pear/pair/pare, its/it's, two/to/too*

ANSWER KEY

1. "adventure travel" and "climate change"
2. Answers will vary. **3.** Answers will vary.
4. Answers will vary: *Floe* refers to the environment and is used when talking about global warming, as there will be more ice floes breaking off and floating with the water flow. Adventure travel requires being flexible, laid back, "going with the flow."

2 Identifying Compound Words

- Read the directions.
- Direct students back to the Strategy box on page 10, to review compound words.
- Remind students that compound words may be hyphenated or not.
- Instruct students to read the article on pages 18–20, including the Introduction.
- After students finish reading, have them fill in the blanks in this activity.
- Have volunteers share the correct answers.

ANSWER KEY

1. 55-year-old
2. 450-mile
3. waterway
4. landscape
5. adventure-travel
6. 26-day
7. coral-reef
8. polar-bear
9. springtime
10. snowfield
11. wildlife
12. bighorn-sheep

Read

- Read the Introduction on page 18 aloud with students or have a student volunteer read it.
- Have students read the passage that follows on pages 19–20 silently within a time limit (10 minutes), or have them read along as you play the audio.
- Tell students to underline any words or phrases that are new or that they don't understand.
- Remind students not to use a dictionary during this part of the lesson.
- Tell students to complete Activity 2 Recalling Information, when they finish the passage.

After You Read

3 Checking Your Comprehension

- Read the directions and ask students to work independently.
- Have students compare their answers with a partner.
- Go over any questions with the whole class.

ANSWER KEY

1. rowboat
2. there was too much ice
3. scuba diving in the coral reefs
4. smaller
5. humpback whales feeding in a channel of water
6. do not have
7. warmer
8. certain kinds of plants and animals

Strategy

Identifying Common Phrases and Idioms

- Read the information in the Strategy box as students follow along.
- Ask students to share any phrases or idioms that they know. Some environmental idioms: *tip of the iceberg, stick in the mud, making waves, down to earth, having your head in the clouds, weathering the storm.*

4 Identifying Common Phrases and Idioms

- Read the instructions.
- Go over the words in the box.
- Have students complete the activity independently and then share their answers with a partner.
- Remind students to cross off the words in the box as they use them.

ANSWER KEY

1. take off
2. has lost count of
3. get defensive
4. in no way
5. top of the world
6. rooting for
7. lead to a boom

5 Focusing on Words from the Academic Word List

- Read the directions with the class.
- Direct students' attention to the academic vocabulary words in the box. Remind students to check off the words as they use them.
- Have students complete the activity and check their answers.
- To verify comprehension, you may wish to have students use the words in a sentence of their own.

ANSWER KEY

1. evidenced
2. emerging
3. resources
4. routes
5. reveal
6. channel
7. founder
8. impact
9. access
10. adapting

6 Guided Academic Conversation

Best Practice

Scaffolding Instruction

This activity requires students to draw on the information they learned in this chapter. When students use their prior knowledge as a scaffold, they can better understand and organize new ideas about topics.

- Divide the class into groups of three
- Read the directions and each of the four items.
- Tell each group to pick three of the four topics to discuss with their group members.
- Have each group assign a reporter for each topic. This person will explain the group's ideas on that topic to the class.
- Be sure to take ample time to have students report a summary of their group's discussions to the whole class.

FOCUS ON TESTING TOEFL® iBT

Analyzing Points of Contrast on Tests

- Read the information at the bottom of page 24 in the Student Book as students follow along.
- Read the instructions for the Practice activity
- Have students read and mark the text as they read.
- Review the answers with the whole class.

ANSWER KEY

1. Canadian
2. Canadian
3. American
4. American
5. American
6. American
7. Canadian
8. Canadian
9. Canadian
10. American
11. Canadian
12. Canadian

REPRODUCIBLE

Expansion Activity

- The purpose of this activity is to practice comparing and contrasting two topics using a Venn diagram.
- Photocopy and distribute the Black Line Master "Comparing Two Countries Venn Diagram," found on page BLM2 of this Teacher's Manual.
- Model a Venn diagram on the board and explain how using a graphic organizer like this will make it easier to compare and contrast two topics/ items. Label one oval "Canada" and the other oval "U.S." Use the information in the passage on page 25 in the Student Book to have the class help you complete the Venn diagram on the board.
- Instruct students to choose a country they know and have them complete a Venn diagram that shows aspects that are different and aspects that are the same as those in the United States.
- Have students explain their diagrams with a partner and then the class. You may wish to post their work on the board.

9 What Do You Think?

- Assign students to small groups.
- Read the questions at the top of page 27 in the Student Book.
- Instruct students to read the passage and the captions for the photos. You may wish to have a volunteer read the passage aloud for the whole class.
- Have students answer the questions within their small group.
- Discuss answers with the whole class.

1 Making Connections

Best Practice

Scaffolding Instruction

Activities such as this will enable students to link recently acquired knowledge with new information they gather from their research.

- Put student in pairs or have them work independently.
- Go over the four research topics and instruct students to choose one on which to work.
- If you have Internet access in your classroom, you may model how the research can be done. Alternatively, you may take your class to the computer lab and guide students' work there.
- Remind students to make notes and to cite where they found the information: the URL and date accessed.
- Have each student or pair report their findings to the class.

Responding in Writing

FOCUS

Writing Tip: Using Details to Support Your Ideas

- Read the Focus box while students follow along.

2 Writing a Paragraph Using Details

- Review the instructions with the class.
- Go over the Steps listed in the activity.
- Once students have chosen their introductory sentence, have them begin their drafts.
- Circulate around the room as they write, answering any questions and offering guidance.
- Remind students to edit and to check spelling, grammar, and vocabulary when they finish.
- You may ask students to share their writing with a classmate and get feedback.
- Collect and review student work. You may wish to post or publish exemplary paragraphs for students to read.

Self-Assessment Log

- Reinforce the advantages of a Self-Assessment Log for students to check their progress.
- Have students check the strategies and vocabulary that they learned.
- Suggest that they review any information that they do not understand. Direct them to find the place(s) in the chapter where the strategy or vocabulary was presented and practiced.
- Address any questions and review strategies and vocabulary as needed.

CHAPTER 2

Teamwork and Competition

In this CHAPTER

Students will focus on teamwork and competition in the areas of sports and business. In the first reading, they will read about soccer player David Beckham, as he describes the teamwork and competition he experienced when he moved from England to Spain. Students will then explore teamwork and competition in the context of business in Part 2 as they read about Kim Ssang Su, a Korean businessman, and his globally competitive company. New vocabulary, reading strategies, and critical thinking will be brought together as students learn test-taking strategies in Part 3.

Chapter Opener

- Direct student's attention to the photo and ask questions: *What kinds of teams are there? Can you be on a team in business? How are business teams the same as sports teams?*
- Read the English proverb aloud and ask students what they think it means.
- Put students in groups and ask them to list the teams they have been a part of and discuss the pros and cons to being on a team.
- Put students in groups and have them discuss the questions in the **Connecting to the Topic** section. (The photo is of David Beckham and Landon Donovan of the Los Angeles Galaxy.)
- Call on groups to recount their discussions with the whole class.

"Two heads are better than one."

English proverb

Chapter Overview

Reading Selections

Beckham: An Autobiography by David Beckham and Tom Watt

Outward Bound by Michael Schuman

Reading Skills and Strategies

Reading without knowing every word

Scanning for numbers

Selecting the main idea of an article

Critical-Thinking Skills

Using a graphic organizer (chain of events diagram) to identify the sequence of events

Recognizing implied feelings

Taking a stand for or against a proposal

Synthesizing Internet content: Taking notes and presenting results

Writing Tip: Describing people by using adjectives

Vocabulary Building

Figuring out idiomatic expressions and specialized terms

Learning sports-related vocabulary

Inferring the meaning of words from context

Understanding metaphors

Using compound adjectives

Inferring the meanings of words as synonyms or antonyms

Focusing on words from the Academic Word List

Focus on Testing TOEFL® iBT

Using strategies to correctly answer multiple-choice questions

Vocabulary

Nouns
- CEO
- factories
- global* brands
- goalkeeper
- goals*
- innovation*
- job*
- mountainside
- net profits
- oldie
- revenues*
- stratosphere
- testing ground
- turnaround
- vigor
- V.P.

Verbs
- ascends
- barks
- cavorts
- chant
- croon
- duplicate
- issuing*
- jumped
- perceived*
- rallying
- sliced
- stoop
- storms
- underestimate*

Adjectives
- chilly
- ear-numbing
- flat-screen
- high-speed
- knee-deep
- leading-edge
- low-cost
- low-end
- nondescript
- odd*
- snow-covered
- tireless
- vicious

Idioms and Expressions
- to be our night
- bracing myself
- chested to chest a ball
- cross it
- cut in
- didn't (don't) really have a clue
- feel at home
- get the drift
- go for goal
- in a comfort zone
- kick-off
- left wing
- midfield
- miss out
- (the) near post
- spurring on
- took (take) a knock or two
- took (take) me off
- touch
- twist in the pit of my stomach
- whisked off

*These words are from the Academic Word List. For more information on this list, see www.victoria.ac.nz/lals/resources/academicwordlist/

Beckham: An Autobiography

Before You Read

Strategy

Figuring Out Idiomatic Expressions and Specialized Terms

- Read the information in the Strategy Box and explain as needed.
- Ask students for examples of specialized terms they know for any sports.
- Write a list of the idioms students provide on the board.

1 Getting the Meaning of Idiomatic Expressions from Context

- Read the directions and explain as needed.
- Model the activity and try to figure out what it means from its context: by reading the first idiom and **Hint**.
- Ask a student to guess the meaning of *took a knock or two* from the **Hint**. Tell students to fill in the correct answer.
- Ask students to guess the meanings of the rest of the idioms and expressions.
- Discuss the answers as a class. Check for comprehension by having students describe a situation in which they might hear the idiom or expression in use. Give students an example, tell students about a time that you *took a knock or two*, such as having a difficult time at a new job or moving to a new city or country.

ANSWER KEY

1. C **2.** A **3.** D **4.** B **5.** D **6.** C
7. A **8.** D **9.** B

2 Getting the Meaning of Specialized Terms from Context

- Read the directions and explain as needed.
- Make sure students understand the completed example.
- Discuss the answers as a class. Check for comprehension by posing questions such as: *What sports have a "kick-off"? What sports have a "left wing"?*

ANSWER KEY

1. e **2.** j **3.** g **4.** c **5.** d **6.** l **7.** k
8. i **9.** h **10.** b **11.** a **12.** f

Read

3 Reading Without Knowing Every Word

- Read the directions and explain as needed.

Content Notes

- Football (or soccer) is the most popular sport in the world today. The first World Cup involved 13 teams and was held in Uruguay in 1930. 32 teams competed in the 2006 World Cup in Germany. To date, the most goals scored in a game is 12 in a World Cup game between Austria and Switzerland in 1954. The final score was Austria 7, Switzerland 5. The first player to ever miss a penalty kick was Valdemar de Brito of Brazil in 1934.
- In the United States, baseball is so popular that it is called "America's National Pastime."
- At the end of the baseball season, there is a round of playoffs in which the best teams of each league compete until the winning team from each league is determined. The two league champions compete in what is called the World Series. The first team to win four of seven games in the World Series becomes the World Series champion.

Reading Tip

Learning Sports-Related Terms

- Direct students' attention to the Reading Tip in the margin and explain as needed.
- Ask students if they are familiar with any sports-related terms in English.
- Tell students to skim the reading passage for sports-related terms in the reading.
- Tell them to choose one and say what they think it means based on its context.
- Read the Introduction or ask a volunteer(s) to read it aloud.
- Discuss the question as a class.
- Have students read the passage silently within a time limit (suggested time limit: 10 minutes).

After You Read

REPRODUCIBLE

Expansion Activity

- The aim of this activity is to give students additional practice with sports-related idioms.
- Make copies of the Black Line Master, "Idiom Puzzles" (BLM 3) and cut the words so each is its own "piece."
- Place the pieces in envelopes and prepare enough envelopes for each pair to have one. Note: The idioms are divided into two sections: idioms from the reading about David Beckham, and baseball idioms. To begin, you may wish to have students work on the soccer idioms alone, and then later the baseball idioms. You may want to spend some time before the activity brainstorming baseball-related idioms as a class. To make the activity more challenging, combine both sets of idioms together.
- Put students in pairs.
- Direct students to close their books and complete this activity without looking back at the reading.
- Explain that they need to put the words together to complete the idioms.
- Call on pairs to read the idioms they put together.
- Write the correct idioms on the board and review the definitions if necessary.

Strategy

Using a Graphic Organizer to Follow the Sequence of Events

- Read the information in the Strategy Box and explain as needed.
- Ask students to recount/recall the first two events that Beckham describes in the reading.

4 Finding the Sequence of Events

- Read the directions and explain as needed.
- Ask students to read the list of key events and complete the chain of events diagram.

ANSWER KEY

Beginning: First Event D F C G B A

End: Last Event E

Best Practice

Organizing Information
Activities such as the chain of events diagram and the sequencing table in the following Expansion Activity will help students organize information from the reading passage so that they are better able to recall the order of events. By having students focus on the order in which things happened, they will not only be able to remember ideas from the reading but also think about them in a logical way.

REPRODUCIBLE

Expansion Activity

- The aim of this activity is to provide students with additional practice with chain of events diagrams.
- Copy and hand out the Black Line Master **Chain of Events Diagram: A Selection from My Autobiography** (BLM 4).
- Tell students that they will now have an opportunity to fill out a chain of events diagram based on an event in their own autobiographies. Ask them to take a few minutes to think of an important event in their own lives, for example getting married, moving to a new country, an accident, etc. and some of the events that occurred during that time.
- Ask them to choose four of the events and write them in the diagram in the correct order. When they have completed their charts, have students share their diagrams in pairs or small groups.

5 Guided Academic Conversation: The Inside Story

- Put students in pairs.
- Ask students to follow the five steps listed in the activity.
- After they have completed the activity, have them compare their lists with those of other classmates.

6 Practicing Speaking by Doing Tasks

Best Practice

Interacting with Others
Activities such as this will help students increase their speaking ability and confidence. By creating a presentation together, students practice explaining their ideas clearly, and understanding those of their partners.

- Put students in pairs. Read the three role-play situations.
- Ask students to choose one of the role-plays and write a dialogue for it.
- Encourage them to incorporate vocabulary and idioms from the reading.
- Allow time for students to perform their role-plays for the class.

7 What Do You Think?

- Have students read the paragraph and discuss the questions that follow.

Content Notes

- The Olympic Games have been the cause of many controversies throughout history. One of the most famous events happened in 1972 when eleven Israeli athletes were kidnapped and killed. The movie, *Munich*, made in 2005, details this event. *Munich* was directed by Steven Spielberg and was nominated for the Academy Award for Best Picture.
- Another well-known film detailing a controversial Olympic event was *Chariots of Fire*. It was made in 1981 and won the Academy Award for Best Picture. *Chariots of Fire* is an English film detailing the true story of two competing British track athletes.

Outward Bound

Before You Read

1 Using the Context to Infer the Meanings of Words

Best Practice

Cultivating Critical Thinking
This type of activity teaches students how to infer the meanings of new words and phrases from their contexts. It also gets them to realize what they may already know about the context and vocabulary.

- Draw student's attention to the *Language Tip* in the margin.
- Read the directions and explain as needed.
- Read the first sentence aloud and ask students to guess the meaning of *CEO* based on the context. Ask the students to complete the rest of the activity.
- Discuss the answers as a class. Check for comprehension: *What's another word for "CEO." What is V.P. an abbreviation for?*

ANSWER KEY

1. C **2.** A **3.** D **4.** B **5.** C **6.** C
7. D **8.** A

Strategy

Scanning

- Read the information in the Strategy Box and explain as needed.
- Ask students to scan a paragraph from the reading and say a number that they found. Their answers will vary.
- Write a list on the board of the numbers called out.

2 Scanning for Numbers

- Read the directions and ask students to work individually.
- Give students 5 minutes to complete the activity.
- Ask volunteers to give their answers.

ANSWER KEY

1. 59 **2.** 35 **3.** 17 billion, 556 million
4. 36.4 billion **5.** 84% **6.** 1996
7. 4.7 billion **8.** 7

Read

- Introduce the reading about Kim Ssang Su by reading the introduction aloud or having a volunteer read it.
- Discuss the questions as a class.
- Set a time limit for students to read the passage (10 minutes).

After You Read

3 Selecting the Main Idea

- Draw students' attention to the Reading Tip in the margin and remind students of what they learned about main ideas in Chapter 1.
- Read the directions and list of possible main ideas.
- Ask students why this statement is better than the other two.

ANSWER KEY

2

Strategy

Understanding Metaphors

- Read the information in the Strategy Box and explain as needed.
- Ask students to find an example of a metaphor in the reading.
- Write a list on the board of the metaphors they find.

4 Understanding Metaphors

- Read the directions and explain as needed.
- Have students complete the activity on their own or with a partner.
- Go over the answers.

ANSWER KEY

Answers will vary. Possible answers:

1. Usage: "Great people! Great company!" he barks. Metaphor: The way Kim shouts is being compared to the barking of a dog.
2. Usage: Revenues jumped 18% last year; Metaphor: The way revenues rose is being compared to something that jumps.
3. Usage: "Great company! Great company!" they chant back. Metaphor: The way the employees respond is being compared to religious chanting.
4. Usage: Kim... cavorts in a mosh pit. Metaphor: The way Kim jumps around is being compared to leaping and prancing.
5. Usage: Kim sliced costs. Metaphor: The way Kim decreased costs is being compared to slicing a piece of cheese with a knife.
6. Usage: He storms about LG's factories and offices; Metaphor: The way Kim visits his factories is being compared to a storm.

Grammar Note

- Another way to compare two things is to use similes. Similes are different from metaphors because they contain the words "like" or "as" and compare two objects. A metaphor does not have the words "like" or "as" and states that one thing is something else. For example, "That boy eats like a pig" is a simile, but "That boy is a pig" is a metaphor. Similarly, "Her legs are like sticks" is a simile, whereas the sentence "Her legs are sticks." means her legs are skinny but is a metaphor because it actually says her legs are another object.

Best Practice

Activating Prior Knowledge

Activities such as this Expansion Activity get students to activate and build on the information they have already learned. Using a topic students are comfortable with enables students to more easily apply new concepts. The following Expansion Activity activates prior knowledge by connecting the familiar topic of friends and family with the new concepts of metaphors and similes.

Expansion Activity

- The aim of this activity is to practice similes and metaphors.
- Tell students they will practice writing their own similes and metaphors.
- Ask students to tell any common similes they know in English or common idioms from their native languages.
- Give examples such as *big as a house, quiet as a mouse, his/her face is as red as a beet, cold as ice, black as night, sleeps like a baby, grows like a weed,* etc.
- Tell students to look at the underlined verbs in activity 4 and think of some new metaphors using the same verbs.
- Have students think about people they know and write sentences using similes to describe their friends and family.
- Ask volunteers to read their sentences.

FOCUS

Using Compound Adjectives

- Read the information in the instruction box and explain as needed.
- Work with students to define *leading-edge gadget*.

5 Using Compound Adjectives

- Read the directions and review the scanning strategy taught earlier in this chapter on page 42.
- Ask the students to match the compound adjectives in the left column with the nouns they modify in the right column.
- Have students give their answers.

ANSWER KEY

1. e **2.** c **3.** a **4.** g **5.** d **6.** b **7.** f

Grammar Notes

- Usually when a compound word is an adjective, it is hyphenated. The compound adjective is placed before the noun in common English word order. If the words are placed after the noun, they are not hyphenated.
- **Hint**: If the words can be separated and retain their meaning, no hyphen is necessary. If the words need to be together to retain the meaning, a hyphen is required.
- Compare:
  The three-year-old child was excited. (When each word in the compound adjective is used alone in the sentence, the sentence doesn't make sense—"The three child…; The year child…; The old child…. Therefore, hyphens are needed when the three are combined.

6 Inferring Meaning: Same or Opposite?

- Define *synonym* and *antonym*. Remind students that a synonym is a word with a similar definition and an antonym is a word with the opposite (or almost opposite) meaning.
- Read the directions and model the first item.
- Ask students to answer the rest of the questions.
- Go over the answers.

ANSWER KEY

1. Antonym	**6.** Antonym	**11.** Antonym
2. Synonym	**7.** Synonym	**12.** Antonym
3. Antonym	**8.** Antonym	**13.** Synonym
4. Synonym	**9.** Antonym	**14.** Synonym
5. Synonym	**10.** Synonym	**15.** Antonym

7 Focusing on Words from the Academic Word List

- Read the directions and explain as necessary.
- Tell students to complete this activity on their own.
- Set a time limit of 5 minutes.
- Review correct answers as a class.
- Check comprehension by asking students to use words in new sentences.

ANSWER KEY

1. odd **2.** job **3.** underestimate **4.** innovation **5.** issuing **6.** goals **7.** perceived

Expansion Activity

- The aim of this activity is to provide further practice with new vocabulary.
- Tell students they will write a vocabulary quiz for the class.
- Have students choose three words from Activity 7.
- For each word, ask them to write a sentence using the word in context. Tell them to make sure the context adequately conveys the word's meaning. Each student will write three sentences.
- Have each student write one of their sentences on the board and draw a blank where the missing vocabulary word should go.
- Have students copy the sentences from the board and fill in the blanks. They should be able to choose the correct vocabulary word based on the context of the sentence.

8 Guided Academic Conversation

Best Practice

Interacting with Others

Activities such as this get students to generate new ideas with the help of their peers and practice expressing their ideas and comprehending and respecting those of others. This type of interaction builds listening and speaking fluency, which is essential to academic success.

- Put students in groups of three.
- Ask them to discuss three of the four topics.
- Tell students to focus on the topic they agree on and write a statement detailing their opinion.
- Have each group share their opinion statement with the class.
- Assign the writing of the opinion statement as homework, or, for variety, as a journal entry.

1 End-of-Chapter Debate

- Write the word *Competition* on one side of the board and *Teamwork* on the other.
- Have students choose to stand beside the word they think is more important.

Best Practice

Organizing Information

Graphic organizers such as T-charts help students organize information in a way that compares and contrasts the topics. By having the class focus on the columns of a T-chart (as in the following Expansion Activity), students will be able to remember ideas from the readings in this chapter. This type of tool is helpful for organizing information in a broad range of academic contexts.

REPRODUCIBLE Expansion Activity

- The aim of this activity is to have students practice using a T-chart to organize their ideas for a debate.
- Copy and hand out the Black Line Master, **Competition/Teamwork T-Chart** (BLM 5).
- Model a T-chart on the board and explain how using a diagram will make it easier to prepare for a debate because the information is organized.
- Group students by the categories they chose in Activity 1, or, to make the activity more challenging, group them by the category opposite to the one they support.
- With their group, they should fill in half of the T-chart with reasons why they support that concept and the other half of the T-chart with reasons why the other concept should not be supported.
- Each group should then write their points on the board and be prepared to discuss their reasoning.
- Discuss which half of the T-chart has more pros and which half has more cons.

2 Making Connections

Best Practice

Scaffolding Instruction

Activities such as this will enable students to link recently acquired knowledge with even newer information they gather from their research.

- Tell students they will look up information on one of the people they have read about.
- Have them choose one of the topics to research.
- Have students share their findings with the class or in small groups.

Responding in Writing

FOCUS

Writing Tip: Describing People by Using Adjectives

- Read the *Writing Tip* and explain as necessary.
- Point out the example and ask volunteers to describe someone using adjectives and examples.

3 Writing and Using Adjectives

Best Practice

Making Use of Academic Content

Brainstorming and developing a paragraph is a concept students will see often throughout their academic careers. Using real-world examples like David Beckham and Kim Ssang Su makes use of topics and tasks found in academic textbooks.

- Read the directions and go over each of the steps explaining as necessary.
- Tell students to work on their own.
- Circulate around the class to check on the progress of each student and offer help as needed.

Vocabulary Note

- Certain suffixes form adjectives; *-y*, *-ful*, *-ing*, *-ive*, and *-able* are common. Examples include *happy*, *funny*, *beautiful*, *fruitful*, *hard-working*, *exciting*, *innovative*, *knowledgeable*, and *capable*. It may help students expand their vocabularies if they know they can add a suffix to a word to make it an adjective.

FOCUS ON TESTING TOEFL® iBT

General Testing Practice

- Read the information in the Focus on Testing section and explain as needed.
- Have students complete the practice activity.
- Go over the answers.

ANSWER KEY

1. C **2.** C **3.** B **4.** D **5.** C **6.** C
7. A **8.** B **9.** A **10.** D

Self-Assessment Log

- Encourage students to maintain a self-assessment log.
- Allow class time so students can check the strategies and vocabulary they learned in the chapter.
- Address any questions and review strategies as needed.

CHAPTER 3

Gender and Relationships

In this CHAPTER

Students will read an informational article that reports about research on personal attractiveness and physical appearance. The second reading contains excerpts from Charlotte Brontë's nineteenth-century novel *Jane Eyre*. The literary passage allows students to dramatize the reading. The topic of gender and relationships lends itself to discussions of the historic and current expectations of personal relationships. Additional activities allow students to expand vocabulary and to practice summary writing. Time is allotted to practice multiple-choice vocabulary test items.

"Life is no longer one's own when the heart is fixed on another."

Hindustan proverb

Chapter Opener

- Put students in small groups to discuss the questions in the **Connecting to the Topic** box.
- Go over the answers as a class.
- For item 3, the ritual means that the person who catches the bouquet will be the next to marry. Ask students if they have a similar custom in their culture.

Chapter Overview

Reading Selections

Being Beautiful or Handsome is Easier Than You Think by Jeremy Nicholson

Jane Eyre (excerpts) by Charlotte Brontë

Reading Skills and Strategies

Skimming for the general idea

Recalling information

Scanning for words with a specific meaning

Presenting a formal reading of a scene from a story

Critical-Thinking Skills

Choosing one point of view over another and defending your choice

Making inferences about a relationship from dialogue

Synthesizing Internet content: Taking notes and presenting results

Writing Tip: Writing down the key points of an article in a summary

Vocabulary Building

Matching phrases to their meanings

Identifying words form the same family

Focusing on words from the Academic Word List

Reviewing vocabulary through pantomime

Focus on Testing TOEFL® iBT

Answering vocabulary questions on tests

Vocabulary

Nouns

- appearance
- attraction
- automaton*
- conventionalities
- dependent
- dissatisfaction
- gender*
- grooming
- medium*
- obsession
- pleasantness
- possessions
- posture
- researchers*
- skeptic

Verbs

- abide
- drawing
- entreat
- sobbing
- summon
- undertake*
- writhed

Adjectives

- attractive
- convinced*
- corresponding*
- frantic
- legible
- obscure
- passionate
- proportionate*
- similar*
- unchanging

Idioms and Expressions

- be shooting for
- go overboard
- the opposite sex
- play a farce
- speak your mind
- statistical analysis*

*These words are from the Academic Word List. For more information on this list, see www.victoria.ac.nz/lals/resources/academicwordlist

Being Beautiful or Handsome is Easier Than You Think!

Before You Read

Strategy

Skimming for the General Idea

- Read the information in the Strategy box.
- Define *general idea* and compare it to the definition of *main idea*. (General idea may be less specific than main idea.)

1 Skimming for the General Idea

- Read the directions aloud.
- Have students work with a partner to create a statement of the general idea of the article.
- Have students compare their general idea with another pair of students and with the class.

2 Matching Phrases to their Meanings

- Review the instructions.
- Remind students to cross off the definitions in the right column as they use them.

ANSWER KEY

1. f **2.** h **3.** g **4.** e **5.** c **6.** b **7.** i
8. d **9.** a

Read

- Have a student volunteer read the Introduction.
- Ask students to keep the questions from the Introduction in mind as they read, as they will discuss them after they read.
- Instruct students to read the passage silently within a time limit (10 minutes) or listen and read as you play the audio.
- Remind students not to use a dictionary during this part of the lesson.

After You Read

3 Identifying Words from the Same Family

- Read the directions aloud.
- Model the first item.
- Instruct students to complete the activity independently.
- Then have students compare their answers with a partner.
- Resolve any questions concerning the correct answers.

ANSWER KEY

1. obsessed **2.** dissatisfaction **3.** passionate
4. attractive **5.** researchers **6.** attraction
7. changeable **8.** pleasantness

4 Recalling Information

- Read the directions and explain as needed.
- Have students work independently.
- Have them compare their answers with a partner.
- Review the correct answers with the class.

ANSWER KEY

1. less
2. high quality clothing
3. standing up straight
4. somewhat attractive
5. somewhat attractive
6. grooming

5 Guided Academic Conversation: Presenting Your Ideas

Best Practice

Interacting with Others

Discussion activities such as these provide students with opportunities to practice their fluency while expressing and explaining their opinions to their classmates. Working in pairs and small groups also allows for a good amount of speaking time for each individual student.

- Review the questions in the Introduction on page 59 of the Student Book.
- Have students share their opinions, now that they have read the article.
- Next, review the four topics in Activity 5 Guided Academic Conversation.
- Assign partners and have each pair select two or three of the topics to discuss with each other.
- Remind students to take notes if needed.
- Combine pairs of students and have students compare their opinions with several other pairs of students.

6 What Do You Think?

Best Practice

Cultivating Critical Thinking

Activities such as this will help students develop the ability to synthesize information from the reading and combine it with their own ideas. This will enable students to better express their opinions about the topic in a clear and logical way.

- Read the directions.
- Have a volunteer read the paragraph "Online Dating."
- Review the four items that follow the paragraph.
- Put students into small groups to discuss the questions.
- You may wish to have some students share their opinions with the whole class, to model the language of opinion-giving.

Jane Eyre (Extract from the classic English novel by Charlotte Brontë)

Introduction to Jane Eyre

- Have students listen as you read the Introduction aloud.
- Clarify any questions from the Introduction.
- Remind students that they may not know all the vocabulary in the reading but should not use a dictionary during this part of the lesson. Meaning can often be found from the context of the reading. After students complete the reading, they may wish to clarify vocabulary that remains unclear.

Before You Read

1 Scanning for Words with a Specific Meaning

Best Practice

Prereading Activities

Before students read a long passage, it is often desirable to focus on several attributes of the reading. This aids student comprehension of the main ideas and important details.

- Before students read the first part of the selection, tell them that they will be doing some prereading activities.
- Read the directions and review the scanning strategy found in Chapter 2, Part 2, if necessary.
- Have students work with a partner to fill in the missing words.
- Review the answers with the class.

ANSWER KEY

1. bridegroom 2. dependent 3. barrier 4. sobbing 5. akin 6. nightingale 7. oath 8. automaton 9. scorn

Strategy

Making Inferences about a Relationship from Dialogue

- Read the information in the Strategy box.
- Clarify as needed.

2 Making Inferences about a Relationship from Dialogue

- Ask a student to read aloud the directions for this activity.
- Have students work with a partner to choose the correct answers and to fill in the blanks.
- Review the correct responses with students.

ANSWER KEY

1. This shows that the two characters are not equal socially because Jane Eyre calls Mr. Rochester "sir" and he calls her "Jane." Therefore, in the society of that time, Jane is subordinate and Mr. Rochester is dominant.
2. This shows that Mr. Rochester feels there is a connection between Jane and him like a string which goes from one heart to the other. However, he believes that once they would be apart, he would suffer and Jane would forget him, but she says that she never should forget him.

Read

- Read the Introduction aloud as students follow along.
- Point out the asterisk after the title of the reading passage. Have students read the note on page 67 in the Student Book where the asterisk is explained.
- Have students read Section 1 silently with a time limit (10 minutes) or have them read and listen as you play the audio.

After You Read

3 Recalling Information (Section 1)

- Instruct students to complete this activity independently.
- Have them compare their answers with a partner.

ANSWER KEY

1. with a lady who lives across the sea **2.** she does not want to be separated from her employer **3.** have been good friends **4.** outside under the stars **5.** she is now very sad about leaving it **6.** original, strong and expanded **7.** she can not be happy if Mr. Rochester's bride lives there **8.** she would never get married to someone she did not truly love as he plans to do

Before You Read

4 Matching Phrases to their Meanings

- Read the instructions aloud.
- Have students complete the activity as best they can before reading Section 2. Encourage them to guess if they aren't sure of the answer.
- Remind students that they can return to this activity after they read the selection and correct their answers. If you choose, you can review the answers after they read the passage.

ANSWER KEY

1. d **2.** f **3.** h **4.** a **5.** g **6.** c **7.** i **8.** b **9.** e

Read

- Have students read Section 2, which continues the conversation between Mr. Rochester and Jane.
- You may play the audio or have students read silently. Encourage them to read to a time limit.

After You Read

5 Recalling Information (Section 2)

- Read the directions.
- Have students complete the activity and compare their answers with a partner.
- Review the correct answers with the class.

ANSWER KEY

1. can go anywhere **2.** a free human being with an independent will **3.** believes that he speaks falsely since he is promised to Miss Ingram **4.** she believes the false rumor that he does not have very much money **5.** Edward **6.** accepts, sir

6 Guided Academic Conversations

- Divide the class into small groups of three or four.
- Instruct one volunteer from each group to read aloud the first of "Two Points of View Concerning Marriage" in the Focus box that follows.
- Instruct students to have a different volunteer read the second point of view.
- Tell the groups that each member of the group will state his or her opinion of the points of view in the Focus box.
- Finally, each group should take a vote to see which point of view is the most popular.
- Groups should appoint a spokesperson to report the group's opinion.
- Conduct a whole class discussion of how the groups agree or disagree.

7 Focusing on Words from the Academic Word List

- Read the directions.
- Remind students to cross off the words as they use them.
- Have students compare their answers with a partner.

ANSWER KEY

1. undertake **2.** similar, corresponding
3. expanded **4.** medium **5.** convinced

REPRODUCIBLE

Expansion Activity

- The purpose of this activity is to have students identify and use prefixes and suffixes with their new vocabulary.
- Photocopy and distribute Black Line Master "Working With Prefixes and Suffixes" found on page BLM6 of this Teacher's Manual.
- Review the instructions with students.
- Remind students that adding a suffix changes the part of speech. Adding a prefix often changes the meaning to the opposite meaning of the word.
- Have students submit their work for your review.

Strategy

Presenting a Formal Reading of a Scene from a Story

- Have students silently read the information in the Strategy box.
- Ask for a volunteer to read each of the numbered points aloud.

8 Presenting a Formal Reading of a Scene from *Jane Eyre*

- Read and explain the directions.
- Assign students to groups of three, paying attention to students' skill levels and the reading demands of the assigned parts.
- Clarify the role of the narrator/stage manager.
- Have students choose their sections and roles, or you may wish to assign them.
- Allow students time to practice until they are comfortable with their reading.
- Have groups present their formal reading to the rest of the class.

FOCUS ON TESTING

Answering Vocabulary Questions on Tests TOEFL® iBT

- Read the information in this section with the class.
- Read the Practice section instructions.
- Do the first item or two with the entire class. Refer back to the pages in the reading selection to find the answers.
- Have students complete the rest of the activity independently.
- Check the answers with the class.

ANSWER KEY

1. D **2.** B **3.** C **4.** B **5.** A **6.** B
7. B **8.** B **9.** A **10.** D

1 Vocabulary Review Using Pantomime

- Write "Actions speak louder than words." on the board and discuss the meaning.
- Define *pantomime* and give examples. You can demonstrate an activity like driving a car or talking on a cell phone.
- Ask volunteers to pantomime drinking something hot or being surprised.
- Read the instructions to Activity 1.
- Divide students into pairs and have them create their list of key words or phrases from the readings. Remind them to be sure that they can act them out.
- When ready, have pairs work together; one pair will pantomime the vocabulary or phrase and the other pair will guess. Have students keep score.

2 Making Connections

- Read the research topics aloud with the class.
- Instruct students to choose one of the topics that interests them for their research on the Internet.
- Have them prepare a presentation for the class.
- Remind students to take notes and write down the URL and date they accessed the information. They should print out photographs or illustrations to show the class.
- Post their research notes and pictures on the board. If students have computer skills, they may wish to prepare a short presentation using technology tools such as PowerPoint® for their presentation.

Responding in Writing

FOCUS

Writing Tip: Writing Down the Key Points in a Summary

- Read the information in the Focus box.
- Ask students for examples of an opinion. Point out that opinions are often preceded by expressions such as *I think, In my opinion, I believe, The way I see it.*

3 Writing a Summary

- Read the directions. Have volunteers read each step of the process.
- Ask student to tell you which reading from the chapter they liked better. Point out that this is an "opinion" and does not belong in a summary.
- If possible, have students work on their summary in class where you can circulate and assist them.
- Put students into small groups to share their summaries when finished. Have them decide whose summary is the most concise and complete.
- Assign revisions as homework.

Self-Assessment Log

- Reinforce the advantages of a Self-Assessment Log for students to check their progress.
- Have students check the strategies and vocabulary that they learned.
- Suggest that they review any elements of the chapter that they do not understand. Direct them to find the place(s) in the chapter where the strategy or vocabulary was presented and practiced.
- Address any questions and review strategies and vocabulary as needed.

CHAPTER 4

Health and Leisure

In this CHAPTER

Students will read about different diets from around the world. In the first reading, they will learn about how what we eat affects us. The second reading explores the notion of ecotourism through the observations of Deborah McLaren, a journalist and director of an international nonprofit program. It also examines the effects that tourists have on the places they visit.

"A good laugh and a long sleep are the best cures in the doctor's book."

Irish proverb

Chapter Opener

- Direct student's attention to the photo and ask questions. *Who are the people in the photo? Where are they?*
- Put students in small groups to discuss the questions in the **Connecting to the Topic** section. (The photo is of an elderly man and a young boy in a garden. They are holding carrots.)
- Read the Irish proverb aloud and ask students what they think it means.
- Put this sentence on the board: *An apple a day keeps the doctor away.* Ask students: *How is this American proverb similar to the Irish one? How is it different?*
- Put students in pairs and ask them to help each other think of proverbs (or other common pieces of advice) from their cultures that address simple ways to maintain good health.
- Call on pairs to report on their discussions to the whole class.

Chapter Overview

Reading Selections

Eat Like a Peasant, Feel *Like a King* by Andrew Revkin

Here Come the Tourists! by Deborah McLaren

Reading Skills and Strategies

Using headings to preview a reading passage

Recalling information

Paraphrasing main ideas

Understanding and analyzing points of view

Distinguishing between fact and opinion

Reading charts for specific information

Critical-Thinking Skills

Using a graphic organizer (a continuum) to rank items

Taking a stand by agreeing or disagreeing

Analyzing points of view

Using a Venn diagram to compare answers from an interview

Reaching a group consensus and writing an opinion statement

Synthesizing Internet content: Taking notes and presenting results

Writing Tip: Structuring an argument to support an opinion

Vocabulary Building

Getting meaning from context

Recognizing synonyms

Scanning for vocabulary

Focusing on words from the Academic Word List

Focus on Testing TOEFL® iBT

Analyzing compound words on vocabulary tests

Vocabulary

Nouns

- affluence
- bargaining
- begging
- benefit*
- cancer
- communities*
- compensation*
- cuisine
- diet
- ecotourism
- fiber
- frontiers
- grain
- heart disease
- hippies
- legumes
- locals
- monounsaturates
- natural resources*
- peasant
- prosperity
- requests
- stinginess
- subculture
- tourists
- treats

Verbs

- acquiring*
- bargained
- distinguish
- flock
- found* (find)
- prevent

Adjectives

- affluent
- annoyed
- demanding
- eclectic
- elite
- enchanted
- inappropriate*
- indigenous
- inexpensive
- peasant
- physical*
- taboo
- up-front

Adverbs

- hence*
- virtually*

*These words are from the Academic Word List. For more information on this list, see www.victoria.ac.nz/lals/resources/academicwordlist/

Eat Like a Peasant, *Feel* Like a King

Before You Read

Strategy

Using Headings to Preview

- Read the information in the Strategy Box and explain as needed.
- Ask students to flip through the chapter quickly and look at the headings. Call on volunteers to tell one of the headings they found. Write a couple of examples on the board and ask students whether they are meant to grab the reader's attention or provide the main idea.

1 Using Headings to Preview

- Read the directions and explain as needed.
- Have students identify the headings from the article and write them down.
- Go over the answers.

ANSWER KEY

1. Early Diets: Nuts and Plants, Why Socrates Loved Olive Oil
2. Early Diets: Nuts and Plants
3. Answers will vary.

2 Getting Meaning from Context

- Read the directions and explain as needed.
- Model the activity. Read the first question under *Getting Meaning from Context*. Ask a student to guess the meaning of the word *peasant* through its relation to the word *king*. Tell students to write the correct answer.
- Have students complete the activity independently.
- Go over the answers.

ANSWER KEY

Possible answers

1. peasant diet = food eaten by poor people
2. elite = the best foods or people
3. eclectic = different, varied
4. affluence = prosperity
5. cuisine = food, cooking

Read

Best Practice

Activating Prior Knowledge

Activities such as this will help students activate their prior knowledge about the topic of the reading passage. In this case, students are asked to think about and discuss what they already know about healthy eating habits and the diets of different cultures.

- Read the Introduction aloud or have a volunteer read it.
- Discuss the questions and any comments.
- Have students read the passage silently within a time limit (10 minutes).

Content Notes

- Vegetarianism became popular in the United States in the 1960s, but it has been around for quite some time. Ancient Hindus and Buddhists, as well as followers of the Greek philosopher Pythagoras and Christian monks of the Renaissance era, have all been known to avoid eating the meat of other creatures for spiritual reasons.
- Veganism is a term that was coined in 1944 by those who were frustrated, for various ethical reasons, by vegetarians who drank milk and ate other dairy products. Consequently, it refers to a lifestyle in which no foods derived from animals are consumed and no products, like fur or leather, made from animals are used.
- The Slow Food Movement was started in Italy, in 1986, by Carlo Petrini. He became concerned that the same processed and fast foods sold the world over would kill many of the existing food traditions. Currently, the nonprofit organization Slow Food USA supports and celebrates American practices like Cajun cooking, the growing of heirloom varieties of fruits and vegetables, the organic raising of animal breeds, and handcrafting wine and beer.
- The Raw Foods Movement was inspired by the notion that our bodies are more suited for the digestion of raw, uncooked foods, as those our ancestors ate before the discovery of fire. It has become popular in recent years.

After You Read

3 Recalling Information

- Read the directions and explain as needed.
- Model the activity by completing the first item as a class.
- Have students complete the activity independently.
- Go over the answers.

ANSWER KEY

1. d **2.** e **3.** a **4.** c **5.** b

Strategy

Paraphrasing Main Ideas

- Read the information in the Strategy Box and explain as needed.
- Make sure students understand the difference between quoting directly and paraphrasing.

4 Paraphrasing Main Ideas

- Read the directions and explain as needed.
- Circulate among the groups and help students as needed
- Go over the answers.

ANSWER KEY

Answers may vary. Possible answers

1. (title) A sure way to feel healthy and energetic is by eating simple foods free of sugar and fat.
2. When people begin to make more money or gain exposure to different lifestyles they abandon traditional diets. Often this may lead to new illnesses.

Strategy

Recognizing Synonyms

- Read the information in the Strategy Box and explain as needed.
- Ask students to think of a pair of synonyms they know.
- Compile a short list on the board.

5 Recognizing Synonyms

- Read the directions and explain as needed
- Have students complete the activity on their own.
- Go over the answers.
- Check comprehension by asking students to use the words in new sentences.

ANSWER KEY

1. c **2.** f **3.** a **4.** e **5.** b **6.** d

Strategy

Organizing Information Using a Continuum

- Read the information in the Strategy Box and explain as needed.
- Draw a sample of a continuum on the board.
- Ask students to think of things that can be rated on a continuum.
- Write their ideas on the board.

6 Ranking Foods on a Continuum

Best Practice

Organizing Information

Activities such as this will help students organize information from the reading passage so that they are better able to synthesize and recall it later. By placing common food items on the numbered list, or continuum, students will be able to remember ideas and details from the reading more easily.

- Put students in pairs.
- Read the directions and explain as needed.
- Ask students for adjectives that describe the foods listed in the vocabulary box (*fattening, natural, processed, etc.*) and write them on the board.
- Have students complete the activity in pairs, using the adjectives to discuss where each food item should be listed.
- Have students compare their answers.

Expansion Activity

- The aim of this activity is to have students create a continuum themselves based on their personal likes and dislikes of certain foods.
- Tell students they will practice organizing different foods on a continuum.
- Designate one end of the room as the "Dislike Very Much" side and the other as the "Like Very Much" side. Explain that all points in between vary from the two extremes.
- Tell students you will call out a food item and they need to line up along the continuum as to how much they like or dislike that food.
- For variation, have students state why they placed themselves where they did on the continuum.
- Discuss how the items on a continuum are not always equally distributed.

7 Take a Stand: Agree or Disagree?

Best Practice

Scaffolding Instruction
When students use their prior knowledge as a scaffold, they can better organize the new concepts presented to them. This activity will help students connect what they have already learned about healthy and unhealthy eating habits to the topics they choose to defend in their debates.

- Put students in small groups.
- Read the directions and explain as necessary.
- Remind students to be prepared to report their positions to the class.

8 Guided Academic Conversation

Best Practice

Interacting with Others
Activities such as this encourage collaborative interaction and authentic conversations. In this case, students are working together to create a TV ad or a menu for a healthy restaurant.

- Read the directions and tasks.
- Put students in small groups and ask each group to choose one task.
- Have groups that chose #1 read their scripts to the rest of the class. Have groups that chose #2 present their menus.

FOCUS ON TESTING   TOEFL® iBT

Analyzing Compound Words

- Read the information in the Focus on Testing section and explain as needed.
- Review the compound nouns studied in Chapter 1.
- Give students time to complete the practice activities.
- Go over the answers.

ANSWER KEY
1. B **2.** D **3.** C **4.** D **5.** C **6.** C

9 What Do You Think?

- Read or ask a volunteer to read the paragraph aloud.
- Put students in small groups to discuss the questions that follow.

10 Discussing Information from a Chart

Best Practice

Cultivating Critical Thinking
Activity 10 provides an opportunity for students to reinterpret data from the chart, synthesize it, and apply it when answering the questions that follow. This type of activity requires students to process the information they have read and express their own ideas and opinions about it.

- Ask students to look at the chart.
- Discuss the answers that follow as a class.

ANSWER KEY
1. **Possible answers:** heart rate and blood pressure drops, carbon monoxide level drops, circulation improves, lung function increases

Here Come the Tourists!

Before You Read

Strategy

Understanding Point of View

- Read the information in the Strategy Box and explain as needed.
- Tell students the next reading is about tourism and that they should try to pay attention to the writer's point of view.

1 Skimming for the Point of View

- Read the directions and explain as needed.
- Have students skim the reading on pages 93–94.
- Ask students which of the three points of view they think is expressed in the article.

ANSWER KEY

2

2 Analyzing the Point of View

- Put students in pairs.
- Read the directions and explain as needed.

3 Getting the Meaning of Words from Context

- Read the directions and model the activity by doing the first item as a class.
- Make sure students understand why "C" is the correct answer.
- Have students complete the activity.
- Go over answers.

ANSWER KEY

1. C **2.** D **3.** A, B **4.** D **5.** B
6. C, B **7.** C, B

Read

- Read the Introduction aloud or ask a volunteer to read it. Explain as needed.
- Discuss the questions as a class.

Content Note

- The mission of the Rethinking Tourism project is to teach people about tourism and create a network of groups who support indigenous peoples. The projects aims to battle the environmental, cultural, social, and economic impacts of tourism that affect communities worldwide.

After You Read

Strategy

Distinguishing Between Fact and Opinion

- Read the information in the Strategy Box and explain as needed.
- Ask students to give examples of facts and opinions.

4 Distinguishing Between Fact and Opinion

- Read the directions and explain as needed.
- Make sure students understand the difference between *fact* and *opinion* statements.
- Have students complete the activity independently.

ANSWER KEY

1. F **2.** F **3.** O **4.** O **5.** O **6.** F **7.** F
8. O **9.** F **10.** F

REPRODUCIBLE

Expansion Activity

- The aim of this activity is to have students practice organize information according to whether it is a fact or an opinion.
- Copy and hand out Black Line Master **Fact and Opinion Organizer** (BLM 7).
- Explain that this chart will help them distinguish between facts and opinions and help them remember details from the reading.
- Assign students a letter: A, B, C, or D. Depending on their letter, that is the paragraph they should use to fill in their Fact and Opinion Organizer.
- After about 10 minutes, have students with the same paragraph assignment work together and compare answers.

5 Scanning for Vocabulary

- Read the directions and explain as needed.
- Tell students to complete this activity on their own.
- Review correct answers as a class.
- Check comprehension by asking students to use the words in new sentences.

ANSWER KEY

1. natural resources **2.** enchanted
3. inappropriate **4.** taboo **5.** acquiring
6. flock **7.** inexpensive **8.** hippie
9. virtually **10.** bargaining

6 Focusing on Words from the Academic Word List

- Read the directions and explain as needed.
- Tell students to complete this activity on their own.
- Go over the answers as a class.
- Check comprehension by asking students to use the words in new sentences.

ANSWER KEY

1. compensation **2.** benefit **3.** communities
4. physical **5.** hence **6.** found **7.** acquiring

Strategy

Using a Venn Diagram to Compare and Contrast

- Read the information in the Strategy Box and explain as needed.
- Tell students to think of two items or ideas that they could compare in a Venn diagram. Answers will vary.

7 Comparing and Contrasting with a Venn Diagram

Best Practice

Organizing Information

Activities such as this will help students organize information from the reading passage so that they are better able to recall important information and talk about it in a logical way. In this case, students are using a Venn diagram to compare and contrast the attitudes and actions of tourists and locals.

- Read the directions and explain as needed.
- Have students scan the article to complete a Venn diagram that compares and contrasts tourists and locals.
- Put students in pairs to compare their diagrams.
- Go over the answers and have students be prepared to explain their choices.

ANSWER KEY

Possible answers: *Circle A*: annoyed, eager for adventure, believe they can contribute, take pictures, give away tokens *Circle B*: enchanted, skilled, playful, up-front, demanding, don't believe tourists can contribute, hate pictures, beg *Middle part C*: think money can help

REPRODUCIBLE

Expansion Activity

- The aim of this activity is to have students compare and contrast their own travel experiences using a Venn diagram.
- Photocopy and hand out the Black Line Master, **Venn Diagram: Comparing Travel Experiences** (BLM 8).
- Ask students to take a couple of minutes to think about a place they have visited, preferably a place that is outside of their country.
- Put students in pairs and tell them to share their travel experiences and impressions of the place they visited; the people who live there, their attitude towards tourists, and the impact they felt tourism had on the place and culture they visited. Tell them to use the questions above the Venn diagram on the Black Line master as a guide.
- Tell students to fill out the differences and similarities between the two places based on their conversations.
- Have each pair present their findings to the class.

8 Guided Academic Conversations

Best Practice

Making Use of Academic Content

Activities such as this will help students develop the ability to separate the ideas presented in the reading from their own ideas about it before they write an opinion statement. Coming to a consensus and writing an opinion statement is an assignment students may encounter in other academic classes.

- Put students in small groups. Read the directions and explain as needed.
- Have students discuss the first topic along with two others.
- Remind them they need to try to reach a group consensus on each topic.
- Call on groups to share their opinion statements.

9 Reading Charts

- Read the directions and explain as needed.
- Put students in small groups to discuss the charts and the questions that follow.
- Go over the answers as a class.

ANSWER KEY

1. They are the most popular tourist destinations, Europe, Answers will vary
2. Chart 1 lists the top 10 countries according to number of tourists that visit, Chart 2 lists the top ten countries based on the money they earn from tourism
3. The amount of vacation days people living in that country have each year, 29, answers will vary

1 End-of-Chapter Game Show

- Read the directions and explain as needed.
- Divide the class into two teams.
- Use the board to keep score.

Expansion Activity

- The aim of this activity is to have students practice arguing the opposing side of a debate question.
- Add a surprise bonus round to Activity 1 in which each team is asked to argue an opposing side of a debate question. This question should build on the factual knowledge the game show has already quizzed students on, but enable them to create a more sophisticated analysis.
- Sample questions: *Are there more advantages or disadvantages to globalization? Can technology be used to protect culture instead of erase it?*
- Have a small group of students serve as judges and give points for every valid argument. Whichever team has more points, wins.

2 Making Connections

- Read the directions and explain as needed.
- Tell them they will look up information on self-improvement fads inspired by international influences on American health and leisure activities.
- Allow students to choose their topics. Instruct them to look at websites on the Internet.
- Have students report their findings to the class.

Responding in Writing

FOCUS

Writing Tip: Structuring An Argument To Support Your Opinion

- Go over the information in the Focus box.
- Point out that an opinion is often based on facts and personal experiences.

3 Writing a Paragraph that Expresses Your Opinion

- Put students in pairs.
- Go over the steps and directions and explain as needed.
- Circulate around the class to check on the progress of each pair.

Self-Assessment Log

- Encourage students to maintain a self-assessment log.
- Allow class time so students can check the strategies and vocabulary they learned in the chapter.
- Tell students to find definitions in the chapter for any words they did not check.

CHAPTER 5

High Tech, Low Tech

In this CHAPTER

Students will focus on different types of technology. In the first reading, they will read about hybrid cars and discuss air pollution. Students will learn how to skim for the general ideas and specialized terms. In Part 2, students will read about "leapfroggers," communities which use information and communication technology that help them move from being agricultural economies to information ones. New vocabulary, reading strategies, and critical thinking will be brought together as students create a study outline, perform interviews, and incorporate ideas in speech and writing.

"Men [and women] have become tools of their tools."

Henry David Thoreau,
U.S. philosopher and writer
(1817–1862)

Chapter Opener

- Have students look at the photo and then work in groups to discuss the questions in the **Connecting to the Topic** section.
- Read the quote aloud and ask students what they think it means.
- Lead the class in discussion and guide the conversation towards technology.
- Ask students: *What kinds of tools do we have today? What kinds of tools existed in Henry David Thoreau's time? Do you think that Thoreau liked technology?*

Chapter Overview

Reading Selections

How Hybrid Cars Work by HybridKingdom.com

Leapfrogging the Technology Gap by Alexandra Samuel

Reading Skills and Strategies

Skimming for the general idea

Scanning for an important word in context to increase your understanding

Identifying the pattern of organization in a reading passage

Outlining the specific details from a reading passage

Analyzing the main point (thesis) of an article

Critical-Thinking Skills

Filling out a chart for comparison

Comparing opinions

Choosing a favorite theme-related item and researching it

Creating a study outline

Interviewing and using a graphic organizer (Venn diagram) to compare answers

Synthesizing Internet content: Taking notes and presenting results

Writing Tip: Selecting strong examples to support a point of view

Vocabulary Building

Inferring the meaning of expressions from context and vocabulary

Inferring the meaning of specialized terms

Understanding compound words

Analyzing compound adjectives with hyphens

Focusing on words from the Academic Word List

Focus on Testing TOEFL® iBT

Using a computer effectively on tests

Vocabulary

Nouns

- benefits*
- best-case scenario
- braking
- carbon footprint
- combustion engine
- components*
- computers*
- craftsmen
- data*
- economy*
- electric motor
- emissions
- four-cylinder engine
- fuel tank
- generator
- hybrid car
- landmarks
- leapfroggers
- marketplace
- network*
- parallel hybrid
- performance
- portion
- propulsion power
- recharging (batteries)
- rpm (revolutions per minute)
- scenario*
- series hybrid
- speeds
- telecenters (also spelled telecentres)
- transmission*
- vehicle*

Verbs

- download
- upload

Preposition

- via*

Adjectives

- efficient
- English-speaking
- global*
- grassroots
- handmade
- Internet-enabled
- Internet-linked
- knowledge-based
- large-scale
- medical*
- parallel*
- service-based
- shocked
- tech-savvy
- well-educated
- widespread*

Expressions

- do our bit
- do their own thing
- on the block

*These words are from the Academic Word List. For more information on this list, see www.victoria.ac.nz/lals/resources/academicwordlist/

How Hybrid Cars Work

Content Notes

- Henry David Thoreau probably used a pen and ink to write. The typewriter was not invented until 1873, 11 years after Thoreau's death.
- Even if the typewriter had existed, Thoreau would not have used one. Thoreau tried to champion nature and fought against materialism. His most famous book is *Walden*, which he wrote in 1854. In *Walden*, he describes the time he spent living alone with nature.

Before You Read

1 Skimming for the General Idea

- Direct students' attention to the Reading Tip in the margin. Review skimming if necessary.
- Read the directions and explain as needed. Remind students not to look up words in their dictionaries.
- Ask students to choose the best general idea.
- Go over the answers.

ANSWER KEY

b

Strategy

Scanning for an Important Word in Context to Increase Your Understanding

- Read the information in the Strategy Box and explain as needed.
- Tell students to take a minute to scan the article and pick one word that is new to them.
- Tell them to quickly scan the article to see if the definition is provided.

2 Scanning for an Important Word in Context

- Read the directions.
- Ask students to complete the activity on their own.
- Go over the answers.

ANSWER KEY

1. because they are more environmentally friendly and reduce our carbon footprint
2. gasoline and electricity (from batteries)

Strategy

Inferring Meaning

- Read the information in the Strategy Box and explain as needed.
- Define the difference between "words" and "expressions." Point out that "educated guess" is a synonym for "inference."

3 Inferring the Meaning of Expressions from Context and Vocabulary

- Read the directions and explain as needed. Ask students to select the best answer.
- Have students complete the activity independently.
- Discuss the answers as a class.

ANSWER KEY

1. B **2.** A **3.** C **4.** A **5.** C **6.** B
7. A **8.** A **9.** B

Read

Best Practice

Activating Prior Knowledge

This Introduction to the reading and the questions that accompany it, give students an opportunity to activate their prior knowledge. In this case, students are asked about their thoughts on air pollution and the perfect car. The discussion questions require students to activate their knowledge on these two topics along with any related vocabulary they have acquired.

- Read the Introduction box aloud, or ask a volunteer to read it.
- Discuss the questions and any comments.
- Have students read "How Hybrid Cars Work" silently within a time limit (10 minutes).

Strategy

Learning Specialized Terms

- Read the information in the Strategy Box and explain as needed.
- Tell students to look back at the reading and choose one specialized term for this topic.
- Compile a list on the board.

4 Inferring the Meaning of Specialized Terms

- Read the directions and model the activity by completing the first item as a class.
- Have students complete the activity independently.
- Go over the answers as a class.

ANSWER KEY

1. g **2.** n **3.** i **4.** h **5.** l **6.** k **7.** m
8. b **9.** j **10.** c **11.** d **12.** k **13.** a **14.** f

Best Practice

Scaffolding Instruction

When students use their prior knowledge as a scaffold, they are better able to organize their ideas about new concepts. The following Expansion Activity requires students to apply what they have already learned about the topic and about distinguishing between facts and opinions in order to complete and discuss the "Fact and Opinion Chart." In this case, students are dealing with facts and opinions about different types of cars.

Reproducible — Expansion Activity

- The aim of this activity is to practice organizing facts and opinions about the reading topic.
- Copy and hand out Black Line Master **Fact and Opinion Chart** (BLM 9).
- Tell students that completing a Fact and Opinion Chart, a type of graphic organizer, will help them separate ideas in the reading from their own thoughts. Define *fact* and *opinion* to make sure students are clear on the difference. Provide examples to clarify as needed, for example, "Exhaust causes the greenhouse effect." (fact) and "SUVs, sports utility vehicles, are unnecessary." (opinion).
- Have students write five facts from the article, "How Hybrid Cars Work" in the "Fact" column of the chart. Then ask them to write their own opinion about each of the facts.
- Allow time for students to share their facts and opinions.

Strategy

Using a Graphic Organizer Chart for Comparison

- Read the information in the Strategy Box and explain as needed.
- Go over how to create a chart.
- Refer to the chart in Activity 5 as an example.

5 Filling Out a Chart for Comparison

Best Practice

Organizing Information

Activities such as this will help students organize information from the reading passage so that they are better able to comprehend it and recall it later. In this case, students are completing a chart according to the qualities of different types of cars.

- Put students in small groups.
- Read the directions and explain as needed.
- Have students complete the chart.
- Discuss the answers as a class.

ANSWER KEY

Quality	Gasoline Car	Electric Car	Parallel Hybrid	Series Hybrid
Has a fuel tank	✗		✗	
Has batteries to store energy		✗	✗	✗
Can operate at speeds of up to 8,000 rpm			✗	✗
Has a range of 50–100 miles		✗		
Runs only on electricity		✗		
Has a generator				✗
Has a four-cylinder engine	✗			
Has both a four-cylinder engine and an electric motor		✗	✗	✗
Has a four-cylinder engine in the trunk (back) area		✗		

Best Practice

Cultivating Critical Thinking

Activities such as the following Expansion Activity, "Automobile Survey," require students to use their critical thinking skills to synthesize the information they gather by interviewing a partner and reporting their findings in a clear and logical way.

REPRODUCIBLE

Expansion Activity

- The aim of this activity is to have students gather information through interviews and report on their findings.
- Copy and hand out Black Line Master, **Automobile Survey** (BLM 10).
- Have students interview five classmates using the chart provided in the Black Line Master to record their classmates' responses.
- Afterwards, have students report their findings. For example, *Four of the five students I interviewed chose their car based on the price.*

6 Talking It Over

Best Practice

Interacting with Others

Pair work activities give students a chance to express their ideas and opinions in authentic conversations while practicing their listening and speaking fluency.

- Put students in pairs. Read the instructions and explain as needed.
- Have students discuss the questions with their partners.
- After they finish, have students compare their answers with those of another pair.

7 Researching a Gadget

- Read the directions and explain as needed.
- If your school has a computer lab, schedule class time for students to do Internet research. Otherwise, assign this activity as homework.
- Schedule time for students to present their gadgets to the class.

Leapfrogging the Technology Gap

Before You Read

Strategy

Identifying the Pattern of Organization in a Reading

- Read the information in the Strategy Box and explain as needed.
- Ask students to name professions in which writing has a structure.
- Review main points and specific details.

1 Identifying the Pattern of Organization

- Read the directions and answer the questions in the direction line as a class.
- Read the rest of the directions together and then have students complete the activity independently.
- Go over the answers as a class.

ANSWER KEY

Pattern 3.

2 Outlining the Specific Details

- Read the directions and explain as needed.
- Ask students to scan the article and identify the examples.
- Go over the answers.

ANSWER KEY

I. Robib, Cambodia
II. Vietnam
III. Bangalore, India
IV. Bolivia
V. Nallavadu a village in Pondicherry, India

3 Analyzing the Main Point (Thesis) of an Article

- Define "thesis" as *an unproven opinion explained in detail and offered as a basis for discussion or argument.*
- Read the directions and explain as needed.
- Model the activity by completing the first item as a class. The two words making up the compound word are "leap" and "frog." The image of frogs jumping over wires represents an economy moving from being agricultural to information.
- Go over the answers.

ANSWER KEY

Possible answer: The image of a frog leaping over another represents how a community can go directly from being an agricultural to an information economy.

FOCUS

Understanding Compound Words

- Read the information in the instruction box and explain as needed.
- Ask students to call out compound words they think of. Answers will vary. Compile a list on the board.
- Review compound words on pages 11 and 88.

4 Understanding Compound Words

- Read the directions and explain as needed.
- Model the activity by completing the first item as a class.
- Go over the answers.

ANSWER KEY

1. A **2.** C **3.** B **4.** B **5.** A **6.** C **7.** A **8.** C

Grammar Note

- Most of the compound words in this activity are common and accepted as permanent. These "permanent" compounds can usually be found in the dictionary and they do not require hyphens.

Expansion Activity

- The purpose of this activity is to have students increase their awareness of compound words and their meanings.
- Ask students to choose an article on a topic that interests them and read it outside of class.
- Tell them that as they read, they should look for compound words. They should break apart the words and/or use the context to help them figure out the meanings.
- Tell them to write down the compound words along with a definition based on the context clues.
- During the next class, put students in groups and have them teach each other the new compound words.
- Call on students to present one or two of their new words to the class.

Read

- Read the Introduction aloud, or ask a volunteer to read it.
- Discuss the questions as a class.
- Have students read the passage within a time limit (10 minutes)

After You Read

Strategy

Creating a Study Outline

- Read the information in the Strategy Box and explain as needed.
- Review roman numerals if necessary.
- Consider showing a sample of an outline to students.

5 Creating a Study Outline

Best Practice

Making Use of Academic Content

In Activity 5, students are creating an outline detailing the key topics and main ideas from the reading. This strategy will enable them to recall information later. Learning to create outlines is a strategy that students will find useful in a wide range of academic courses.

- Read the directions and have students complete the outline.
- Remind students that this is an independent activity.
- Go over the answers.

ANSWER KEY

I. Location: *Robib, Cambodia*

1. *Motorcycles are Internet-enabled. They carry information between remote villages and central computer hubs.*

II. Location: *Vietnam*

1. *knowledge-based*

III. Location: Bangalore, India

1. interlocking programming *shops*
2. call *centers*
3. *tech companies*

IV. Location: Bolivia

1. *a rural radio station uses the Internet to research information*

V. Location: Nallavadu, a village in Pondicherry, India

1. *village's telecentres*
2. *used as a community alarm during the* tsunami *of 2004*

FOCUS

Understanding Compound Adjectives

- Read the information in the instruction note and explain as needed.
- Ask students to take a minute to scan the reading and find examples of compound adjectives.
- Make a list on the board.

6 Analyzing Compound Adjectives with Hyphens

- Read the directions and explain as needed.
- Model the activity and do the first item as a class.
- Have students complete the activity independently.
- Go over the answers.

ANSWER KEY

Possible answers: 1. motorcycles that can access the Internet **2.** an economy based on services rather than goods **3.** factories that produce goods on a large scale, in large quantities **4.** an economy that is based on information and/or knowledge **5.** the best course of action possible **6.** people who have a high-level of education; programmers who know a lot about technology **7.** people with a high level of education, who know a lot about technology and speak English **8.** a center where communication is connected to the Internet

7 Focusing on Words from the Academic Word List

- Read the directions and explain as needed.
- Have students complete the activity independently.
- Have students refer back to the reading passage to check their answers.
- Go over the answers as a class.
- Check comprehension by asking students to use words in new sentences.

ANSWER KEY

1. medical **2.** economy **3.** global **4.** benefits **5.** via **6.** network **7.** computers **8.** vehicle **9.** data **10.** data **11.** transmission

Talking It Over

8 Discussing Information Technology

- Put students in small groups to discuss the questions.
- After they have finished, have them compare their answers with those of another group.
- Call on students to share their answers.

9 What Do You Think?

- Put students in small groups.
- Ask them to read the short paragraph called "Using Cellular Phones" and discuss the answers that follow.
- Call on groups to share their answers with the class.

1 Guided Academic Conversation

- Direct students' attention to the *Culture Note* about *blogs* in the margin of page 123.
- Go over the directions and steps and explain as needed.
- Put students in pairs to complete the interviews.

REPRODUCIBLE Expansion Activity

- The purpose of this activity is to provide students with additional topic-related research practice.
- Photocopy and hand out the Black Line Master ***Blog* Research Chart** (BLM 11)
- Tell students that they are going to research a blog on a topic that interests them, such as a hobby, sport, place of interest, etc.
- Tell them they can type in "*blog search*" in the search engine to find *blogs* on various topics.
- Tell them to fill out the chart from the Black Line Master as they do their research.
- Allow time during the next class for students to present their *blogs*.

2 Making Connections

- Read the instructions and explain as needed.
- Tell students to select a topic to research on the Internet.
- If you have access to a computer lab, schedule this as a lab activity. Otherwise, assign it as homework.

Responding in Writing

FOCUS

Writing Tip: Selecting Strong Examples to Support Your Point of View

- Read the Writing Tip and explain as needed.
- Ask students whether they feel technology has had a positive or negative impact on modern society.
- Ask students to think of a strong example to support their opinion.

3 Writing About Technology

- Go over the directions and the steps and explain as needed.
- Have students complete the writing task independently.

FOCUS ON TESTING TOEFL® iBT

Using a Computer on Tests

- Present the information in the Focus on Testing section and explain as needed.
- Allow time for students to complete the practice activities.
- Go over the answers.

ANSWER KEY

1. mouse **2.** adaptive **3.** linear **4.** table **5.** directions **6.** drag and drop **7.** glossary **8.** timer **9.** notepaper

Self-Assessment Log

- Encourage students to maintain a self-assessment log.
- Allow class time so students can check the strategies and vocabulary they learned in the chapter.
- Tell students to find definitions in the chapter for any words they did not check.

CHAPTER 6

Money Matters

In this CHAPTER

Students will focus on financial matters in both business and in personal situations. In the first reading, they will learn about a small business in Spain that grew into a global success. Students will learn how to scan for specific information and recognize word families. In Part 2, students will read a short story by William Somerset Maugham that focuses on the embarrassment that a lack of money can cause in a social situation. New vocabulary, reading strategies, and critical thinking will be brought together as students research, discuss, and diagram their ideas.

> "One coin in an empty moneybox makes more noise than when it is full."
>
> Arabic proverb

Chapter Opener

- Draw students' attention to the photograph and ask questions. *Look at the woman in the photo. Who do you think she is? What do you think she does for work?*
- Put students in groups and have them discuss the questions in the **Connecting to the Topic** section.
- Read the Arabic proverb aloud and ask students what they think it means.
- Ask students: *Does the Arabic proverb mean that it is okay to not have much money? How much money do you need to survive? How much money do you need to buy something you want?*
- Put students in groups and ask them to discuss any proverbs about money from their own culture.

Chapter Overview

Reading Selections

Executive Takes Chance on Pizza, Transforms Spain by Stephen Wade

The Luncheon by William Somerset Maugham

Reading Skills and Strategies

Scanning for specific information

Checking comprehension with multiple choice questions

Identifying the setting, characters, and conflict in a narrative

Predicting events in a narrative

Using a timeline to recall the series of events in a plot

Critical-Thinking Skills

Comparing opinions

Synthesizing Internet content: Taking notes and presenting results

Analyzing the actions and outcomes of a situation and presenting an alternative solution through a skit

Solving problems related to the theme

Writing Tip: Making a cluster diagram to help organize ideas

Vocabulary Building

Recognizing word families

Getting the meaning of words from context

Focusing on words from the Academic Word List

Focus on Testing TOEFL® iBT

Reading between the lines on reading comprehension tests

Vocabulary

Nouns

- boom
- chain (as in a group of similar businesses)
- convenience
- drama*
- executive
- franchises
- globalization*
- growth markets
- management
- mentality*
- outlets (as in individual businesses in a chain)
- pizzeria
- projected sales
- specialties
- untapped market

Verbs

- anticipated*
- flattered
- found* (find)
- maturing*
- modernizing
- prospered
- startled
- transform*

Adjectives

- affordable
- amicable
- effusive
- enormous*
- imposing*
- inadequate*
- inclined*
- marketing
- mortifying
- multinational
- succulent
- vindictive

Adverb

- absentmindedly

*These words are from the Academic Word List. For more information on this list, see www.victoria.ac.nz/lals/resources/academicwordlist/

Executive Takes Chance on Pizza, Transforms Spain

Before You Read

Strategy

Previewing a Reading

- Read the information in the Strategy Box, and explain as needed.
- Ask the students to look at the title and state what they think the general idea of the reading will be.
- Answers may vary. Possible answers may include *Businessman starts pizza business, Executive opens pizzeria, New pizza restaurant in Spain.*

1 Scanning for Specific Information

- Read the directions and focus students' attention on the title again.
- Give students one minute to scan the reading.
- Have students answer the questions independently.
- Put students in small groups or pairs to compare answers.

ANSWER KEY

Possible answers:

1. Leopoldo Fernandez
2. decides to try something new
3. modernizes, adds convenience, Answers will vary.

Strategy

Recognizing Word Families

- Read the information in the Strategy Box, and explain as needed.
- Look at the examples provided, *combine, combined*, and *combination.*
- Point out the word *transform* from Activity 1. Ask students if they know the noun form of the word *(transformation).*

2 Recognizing Word Families

- Read the directions, and explain as needed.
- Ask the students to fill in the related words from the reading.
- Go over the answers as a class.

ANSWER KEY

1. globalization	6. prospered
2. pizzeria	7. specialties
3. convenience	8. affordable
4. modernizing	9. mentality
5. management	10. maturing

Grammar Notes

Certain suffixes always make words the same part of speech. The suffixes **-ance/-ence, -hood, -ity, -ment, -ness, -ship,** and **-tion/-sion** all change words to nouns. The new words are in the same family but are different parts of speech.

- **-ance/-ence** changes adjectives (and sometimes verbs) into nouns: *silent/silence, appear/appearance*
- **-hood** changes nouns into other forms of nouns: *child/childhood*
- **-ity** changes adjectives into nouns: *possible/possibility*

- **-ment** changes verbs (and sometimes adjectives) into nouns: *enjoy/enjoyment, merry/merriment*
- **-ness** changes adjectives into nouns: *open/openness* (noun).
- **-ship** changes nouns into other forms of nouns: *friend/friendship*
- **-tion/-sion** changes verbs into nouns: *describe/description, decide/decision*

Students should notice that sometimes other changes are made to the root word before the suffix is added.

Best Practice

Organizing Information

The following Expansion Activity gets students to use a cluster diagram to help them organize and build vocabulary. This activity requires students to reflect on what they have learned about word families and apply it as they complete their cluster diagrams.

REPRODUCIBLE

Expansion Activity

- The aim of this activity is to have students practice noun suffixes.
- Copy and hand out Black Line Master **Noun Suffix Clusters** (BLM 12).
- Explain that students should fill each center circle with a common noun suffix.
- Allow enough time for students to complete each cluster by filling in the smaller circles with root words that take the noun suffix.
- Go over answers and have students share clusters.

Read

- Read the Introduction aloud or ask a volunteer to read it.
- Discuss the questions as a class.
- Have students read the passage silently within a time limit (10 minutes).

Content Note

- In the United States, Pizza Hut started small, just as TelePizza did. It has often been named the Best Pizza Chain in America as voted by consumers. Two brothers and their mother turned just $600 into the world's largest pizza company. They opened the first Pizza Hut in Wichita, Kansas.

After You Read

3 Getting the Meaning of Words from Context

- Read the directions and model the activity by doing the first item as a class.
- Have students complete the activity on their own.
- Discuss the answers as a class.

ANSWER KEY

1. promoting the buying and selling of products **2.** used in and/or existing in many nations or countries **3.** estimated sales **4.** business locations **5.** a company with many stores selling the same product **6.** a quick and significant increase **7.** a part of the business that has not been explored yet **8.** chains that are owned by individuals **9.** a market that has potential to grow

Best Practice

Scaffolding Instruction

The following Expansion Activity gets students to draw on what they learned from the reading passage and combine that with their own ideas and experiences in order to come up with a marketing plan. When students use their prior knowledge as a scaffold, they are better able to organize their ideas and apply them to new concepts.

REPRODUCIBLE

Expansion Activity

- The aim of this activity is to have students create a mini marketing plan for their own pizza company.
- Tell students they will start their own pizzeria.
- Copy and hand out Black Line Master **Pizzeria Marketing Plan Outline** (BLM 13).
- Put students into small groups and tell them they've been given enough money to open their own restaurants.
- Allow them enough time to prepare a marketing presentation for the other groups. Consider bringing in a sample marketing plan from a local restaurant.
- Tell students their presentations should be approximately 5–10 minutes in length and include the name of their pizzeria, the kinds of pizza and services they will offer, menu costs, décor of the restaurant, and what makes them different from all the other pizzerias in town.
- Have each group present their marketing plan to the class.

4 Checking Your Comprehension

- Read the directions.
- Have students complete the activity on their own.
- Go over the answers as a class.

ANSWER KEY

1. B **2.** C **3.** A **4.** C **5.** B **6.** C

5 Guided Academic Conversation: Globalization and How It Affects Us

Best Practice

Interacting with Others

Activities that involve group discussions give students an opportunity to practice expressing their ideas about different topics while increasing their listening and speaking fluency. In this case, students are discussing issues having to do with fast food, chain stores, and owning one's own business.

- Put students in small groups and read the directions.
- Have them discuss the issues in their groups.
- After they have finished, have each group join another group to compare their answers.

6 Making Connections

- Read the directions, and explain as needed.
- Have students look up "TelePizza" on the Internet or at the library.
- If your program has a computer lab, you can schedule class time for students to do Internet research, or you can assign this activity as homework.
- Ask students to answer the questions in the student book and prepare their answers in a 3–5 minute presentation.
- Schedule time for students to report their findings during the next class.

FOCUS ON TESTING TOEFL® iBT

Reading Between the Lines

- Read the information in the Focus on Testing section, and explain as needed.
- Have students work independently to read the passages and select the best answers.
- Go over the answers.

ANSWER KEY

1. C **2.** D **3.** B

7 What Do You Think?

- Put students in groups. Read the directions.
- Allow time for students to read the paragraph and answer the questions.
- Discuss the answers as a class.

The Luncheon

Before You Read

Strategy

Identifying the Setting, Characters, and Conflict in a Narrative

- Read the information in the Strategy Box, and explain as needed.
- Ask students to name the setting, characters, or plots in a favorite story.

1 Identifying the Setting, Characters, and Conflict

- Read the directions.
- Give students time to skim the first few paragraphs of the reading and answer the questions.
- Go over the answers.

ANSWER KEY

Possible answers:

1. in the 1930s, Paris
2. a writer, a woman
   Woman: wealthy, forty, imposing, talkative
3. the restaurant is more expensive than main narrator can afford

2 Getting the Meaning of Words from Context

- Read the directions.
- Model the activity by looking at the first adjective and the answer.
- Have students finish the other questions.
- Go over the answers.

ANSWER KEY

1. B **2.** A **3.** B **4.** A **5.** C **6.** A **7.** C
8. B **9.** B **10.** C

Read

Strategy

Predicting Events in a Narrative

- Read the information in the Strategy Box, and explain as needed.
- Ask students to talk about movies they have seen or stories they have read which had endings that surprised them.

3 Predicting Events in a Narrative

- Read the directions.
- Have students make a prediction about the story based on the first few paragraphs they skimmed for Activity 2 (pages 139–141).
- List students' predictions on the board and revisit them after they have finished reading.

REPRODUCIBLE

Expansion Activity

- The aim of this activity is to have students practice making predictions about their own futures.
- Prepare note cards for the students from the Black Line Master **Futures** (BLM 14).
- Tell students they will now have a chance to predict their own futures.
- Hand out one index card to each student.
- Explain to students that they should predict where they think they will be in one year.

- Collect the cards and read them out loud.
- Distribute another set of cards but this time ask students to predict where they will be in 5 years. (You can vary this activity by changing the number of years.)
- Read the cards out loud without reading the students' names. Ask other students to guess whose prediction each is.
- Distribute the cards that ask them to predict where they will be in 10 years and repeat.

Introduction

- Now read the Introduction aloud or ask a student to read it.
- Discuss the questions in the Introduction as a class.
- Have students read the story within a time limit (15–20 minutes).

Vocabulary Note

- This is a lengthy reading with a great deal of vocabulary. Remind students they will not need to understand every word in order to understand the story. Although essential vocabulary is taught in the pre-reading, consider taking additional time after the reading to go over additional new vocabulary words.

Content Note

- The Latin Quarter is a historic Paris neighborhood. The streets are narrow and it is this quarter where a tourist can find typical Parisian cafés, lots of students, bars, restaurants, and theaters.

Expansion Activity

- The aim of this activity is to give students additional practice with new vocabulary words.
- Distribute index cards or small pieces of paper to students.
- On the card or paper, students should write a word from the short story that is new to them. Let them know they should choose a word that has not been covered in class or in a previous activity.
- On the other side, students should write a definition of the unknown word based on its context.
- Collect the cards and go over them with the rest of the class.
- Encourage students to make a set of cards with words that are important to them.

After You Read

FOCUS

Understanding the Plot: Recalling the Series of Events

- Read the information in the instruction note and explain as needed.
- Ensure that students understand the terms *plot*, *framework tale*, and *flashback*. Students should know that *plot* is the series of events, *framework tale* is a story inside another story, and *flashback* is a tool used to describe an event that happened before this point in the story.

4 Understanding the Plot: Recalling the Series of Events

- Point out the Reading Tip in the margin.
- Read the directions and have students complete the diagram.
- Have students complete the activity independently.
- Go over the answers.

ANSWER KEY

E, D, G, H, B, F, A, C

5 Focusing on Words from the Academic Word List

- Read the directions, and explain as needed.
- Tell students to complete this activity on their own.
- Have students refer back to the reading passage to check their answers.
- Go over the answers as a class.
- Check comprehension by asking students to use the words in new sentences.

ANSWER KEY

1. imposing
2. inclined
3. anticipated
4. enormous
5. drama
6. found
7. inadequate

Guided Academic Conversation

6 Creating a Skit

- Put students in pairs. If possible, pairs should be one female and one male.
- Have students read the question and write a dialogue to illustrate what the man might have said.
- Have each pair perform their skit for another pair.
- Discuss the various solutions as a class.

7 Solving Problems

Best Practice

Cultivating Critical Thinking

This type of discussion activity requires students to use critical thinking skills such as inferring meaning, hypothesizing, analyzing, and drawing conclusions.

- Put students into groups of four.
- Ask them to discuss the list of questions.
- Tell students that they will present the rule they develop in question 5 to the class.
- Have the class vote on which group developed the best rule.

1 Making Connections

- Read the directions, and have students choose one of the topics to research on the Internet.
- If your program has a computer lab, you can schedule class time for students to do Internet research, or you can assign this activity as homework.
- Schedule time during the next class for presentations.

Responding in Writing

FOCUS

Writing Tip: Making a Cluster Diagram

- Read the Writing Tip, and explain as needed.
- Explain that the diagram on page 151 is based on a quote by Bill Gates, one of the founders of Microsoft Corporation.

2 Using a Cluster Diagram to Organize Ideas and Write a Paragraph

Best Practice

Making Use of Academic Content
This activity requires students to go through the various steps of the process involved in writing a well-organized paragraph. By completing the steps in this activity, students practice some of the strategies that will help prepare them with the types of writing assignments they will encounter in a variety of academic contexts.

- Read the directions and the quotes, and go over the steps in the activity.
- Have students complete the activity on their own.

Self-Assessment Log

- Encourage students to maintain a self-assessment log.
- Allow class time so students can check and review the strategies and vocabulary they learned in the chapter.
- Tell students to find definitions in the chapter for any words they did not check.

CHAPTER 7

Remarkable Individuals

In this CHAPTER

Students will focus on the qualities that make people remarkable. In the first reading, they will learn about Confucius, who has had a profound influence on society for over 2,500 years. Students will learn how to skim for the general idea and figure out words from structure clues. In Part 2, students will read about five heroes who are courageous enough to fight for the rights and dignity of the oppressed. Students will learn that heroes come from all continents and backgrounds. New vocabulary, reading strategies, and critical thinking will help students research, discuss, and organize their ideas.

"A good reputation sits still; a bad one runs about."

Russian proverb

Chapter Opener

- Direct students' attention to the photo and have them work in small groups to discuss the questions in the **Connecting to the Topic** section. (The photo is of an elderly volunteer tutoring a young girl in math.)
- Read the Russian proverb aloud and ask students what they think it means.

Chapter Overview

Reading Selections

Confucius, 551 B.C.E.*–479* B.C.E. by Michael H. Hart

Courage Begins with One Voice by Kerry Kennedy

Reading Skills and Strategies

Skimming for the general idea

Identifying key terms

Previewing to determine organization

Identifying the voices in a reading

Critical-Thinking Skills

Supporting or disproving a general statement with facts

Expressing an opinion

Using a graphic organizer (a continuum) to rank leaders

Comparing ideas

Synthesizing Internet content: Taking notes and presenting results

Writing Tip: Using a Venn diagram to compare and contrast two topics

Vocabulary Building

Figuring out meaning from structure clues: compound words, prefixes, and suffixes

Forming new words from the same word family

Matching words to their definitions

Using expressive synonyms

Creating new words using noun suffixes

Focusing on words from the Academic Word List

Focus on Testing TOEFL® iBT

Understanding sentence-insertion questions on tests

(Reading: *The Most Dangerous Jobs in the U.S.*)

Vocabulary

Nouns

- assistance*
- atrocities
- background
- childhood
- commitment*
- commoners
- cornerstones
- decisions
- defender
- demilitarization
- dynasty
- eloquence
- energy*
- etiquette
- expression
- (the) Golden Rule
- holocaust
- innovator*
- investment*
- lament
- negotiations
- notions*
- obstacles
- outlook
- perception*
- preparation
- prestige
- principality
- promotion*
- repression
- responsibility
- role*
- servitude
- tyranny
- valor
- violations*

Verbs

- atone
- conduct*
- eradicate
- founded*
- modernize
- monitors*
- permeated
- reared
- resigned
- sacrifice
- seized
- strive
- suppress

Adjectives

- benevolent
- civil*
- compelling
- Confucian
- depressed*
- diligent
- enduring
- governmental
- influential
- medical*
- overwhelming
- philosophical*
- political

Adverbs

- easily
- primarily*

Expression

- take up the torch

*These words are from the Academic Word List. For more information on this list, see www.victoria.ac.nz/lals/resources/academicwordlist/

Confucius, 551 B.C.E.–479 B.C.E

Before You Read

1 Skimming for the General Idea

- Go over the directions.
- Review the Strategy Box for skimming covered on page 58.
- Tell students to skim the reading and fill in the bubble of the best general idea of the reading.
- Take a vote, by show of hands, to see which statement students feel best expresses the overall idea of the reading.
- Have students state why they chose the statements they did.

ANSWER KEY

C

Strategy

Figuring Out Words from Structure Clues

- Read the information in the Strategy Box, and explain as needed.
- Review compound words and suffixes as needed.
- Look at the examples provided in the box and ask students if they can think of any other examples of words like these. Provide a couple of examples, such as *headache*, *basketball*, and so on, to help them.

2 Figuring Out Words from Structure Clues

Best Practice

Activating Prior Knowledge

Activity 2 asks students to draw on the vocabulary they already know in order to figure out the meanings of compound words. By drawing on the vocabulary they already know, students are better able to figure out new words and read more fluently.

- Read the directions and do the first item as a class.
- Ask the students to complete the activity independently.
- Call on students to share their answers.

ANSWER KEY

Possible answers:

1. the shared condition of being children
2. a person's past, things someone has done in the past
3. territory ruled by a prince
4. the main ideas that support a philosphy
5. wanting to do good
6. someone who defends
7. look at things/the way you see things
8. one who starts new things
9. are common, not rich

Grammar Notes

Certain suffixes always make words the same part of speech. Refer to the Grammar Notes on noun suffixes in Chapter 6. Some suffixes are common adjective endings; **-able**, **-al**, **-en**, **-ful**, **-ic**, **-ive**, **-less**, **-ous**, and **-y**, all convert words into adjectives. The new words are in the same family but are different parts of speech.

- **-able** changes verbs or nouns into adjectives: *like/likeable, pleasure/pleasurable*
- **-al** changes nouns into adjectives: *finance/financial*
- **-en** changes nouns into adjectives: *wood/wooden*
- **-ful** changes nouns into adjectives: *beauty/beautiful*
- **-ic** changes nouns into adjectives: *scene/scenic*
- **-ive** changes verbs into adjectives: *select/selective*
- **-less** changes nouns into adjectives: *power/powerless*
- **-ous** changes nouns into adjectives: *fame/famous*
- **-y** changes nouns into adjectives: *rain/rainy*

Students should be made aware that sometimes other changes are made to the root word before the suffix is added. See the following vocabulary note.

Vocabulary Notes

Adding prefixes and suffixes can affect the spelling. Some common ideas to share with students include:

- Most prefixes do not alter the spelling of the word; the prefix can simply be added. Some exceptions are **ad-**, **com-**, and **in-**. For example, *legal* becomes *illegal* instead of *inlegal*. The last letter in the prefix changes to match the beginning consonant of the root.
- If a one-syllable root ends in a vowel and a consonant, double the final consonant before adding a suffix that begins with a vowel. For example, *run* becomes *running*.

Read

- Read the Introduction aloud or have a volunteer read it.
- Discuss the questions as a class.
- Have students read the passage silently within a time limit (10 minutes).

Content Notes

- Confucius's books have sold over 18 million copies in China.
- Shih Huang Ti was the first emperor in China. He founded the Chin dynasty from which China's name is taken. Although many good things happened during his reign (a network of roads was built, units of weights and coins were standardized), a lot of bad things also happened during his reign. For example, books that did not conform to Chin philosophy were burned and scholars who conformed to more traditional beliefs were buried alive. The dynasty collapsed four years after his death.

After You Read

3 Identifying Key Terms

- Model the activity by doing item 1, *The Analects* and ask students to choose the best match. Allow them to scan the reading to read the term in context.
- Have students complete the activity individually.
- Discuss the answers as a class. Check for comprehension by having students write sentences using the vocabulary.

ANSWER KEY

1. c **2.** g **3.** d **4.** b **5.** f **6.** e

Best Practice

Scaffolding Instruction

The following Expansion Activity, gets students to rely on their own experiences and use new vocabulary learned in this chapter in order to express their own philosophies. This activity and the discussion it promotes allows students to synthesize the material they have learned thus far in the chapter.

REPRODUCIBLE Expansion Activity

- The aim of this activity is to promote theme-based group discussions
- Copy and hand out Black Line Master, **Confucious Says, We Say** (BLM 15).
- Tell students they will have a chance to state their own philosophies.
- Put students into small groups of four. Encourage them to discuss what Confucius's philosophies (listed in the left column) mean to them.
- Then have the groups write their own philosophies in the right column and present them to the other groups.

4 Forming New Words from the Same Word Family

- Read the directions and discuss the answer for item 1.
- Have students complete the rest of the activity.
- Move around the classroom to ensure that students are following the instructions.
- Go over the answers.

ANSWER KEY

1. enduring **2.** influential **3.** easily
4. political **5.** primarily **6.** governmental
7. Confucian **8.** philosophical **9.** modernize

REPRODUCIBLE Expansion Activity

- The aim of this activity is to provide practice with word families.
- Copy and hand out Black Line Master **Word Family Charts** (BLM 16).
- Explain that students should fill out a chart for root words and change the prefixes and suffixes to create several words from the same family.
- Go over the answers for the chart that is started for them on the worksheet.
- Challenge them to create two more charts on their own.
- Go over the answers and have students share their charts.

5 Matching Words to Their Definitions

Best Practice

Cultivating Critical Thinking

Vocabulary activities such as this one require students to apply their critical thinking skills in order to infer the meanings of vocabulary words they are not sure about. In this case, students need to scan the reading for the words they are not sure about and use the context to help infer their meanings. This activity teaches students to use a strategy that they can apply to a broad range of contexts, both inside and outside of the classroom.

- Read the directions and model the activity by doing the first item as a class.
- Have students complete the activity independently.
- Go over the answers.

ANSWER KEY

1. j **2.** e **3.** n **4.** a **5.** h **6.** l **7.** k **8.** o
9. c **10.** f **11.** m **12.** b **13.** g **14.** i **15.** d

Expansion Activity

- The aim of this activity is to practice new vocabulary items.
- Tell students they will write a vocabulary quiz for the class.
- Have students choose three words from Activity 5 on page 158.
- For each word, ask them to write a sentence using the word in context. Tell them to make sure the context adequately conveys the word's meaning.
- Each student should write one of their sentences on the board and draw a blank line indicating where the vocabulary word should go.
- Have students copy the sentences from the board and fill in the blanks. They should be able to choose the correct vocabulary word based on the context of the sentence.

Strategy

Finding Facts to Support or Disprove General Statements

- Read the information in the Strategy Box, and explain as needed.
- Ask students to define "fact." Give the example *Earth is the third planet from the sun.*
- Ask the difference between "fact" and "opinion."

6 Finding Facts to Support or Disprove General Statements

- Put students in small groups and read the directions.
- Have them discuss the statements and decide whether or not they are true or false.
- When they have finished, have them compare their ideas with those of another group.

ANSWER KEY

1. T, He was reared in poverty and had no formal education.
2. F, Through diligent study, he educated himself and became a learned man.
3. T, For two thousand years his concept of government, and his ideas about personal conduct and morality permeated Chinese life and culture. Even today, his thoughts remain influential.
4. T, He was the first major philosopher to state the Golden Rule, "Do not do unto others that which you would not have them do unto you."

7 Guided Academic Conversation

- Put students into small groups to discuss the questions.
- Call on students to share their answers and drawings with the class.

8 What Do You Think? Rating Leaders

Best Practice

Making Use of Academic Content
Activities such as this help students develop and practice research skills. Learning how to do effective, accurate research is a valuable skill that students will find applicable in a variety of academic and professional contexts.

- Read the directions and prepare students for research.
- Schedule time in the school's computer lab for this activity or assign it as homework.
- Schedule time during the next class for students to share their information on the leaders they researched.

9 Rating Leaders Using a Continuum Graph

Best Practice

Organizing Information
Rating information on a continuum graph helps students grasp concepts and organize them in a format that will allow them to process and recall the information they have learned more easily.

- Read the directions, and explain as necessary.
- Compile a list of the leaders students researched for Activity 8.
- As a class, place the leaders on a continuum according to how much harm or good the class thinks they have done. Try to reach as much of a consensus as possible.
- Discuss the questions that follow the continuum graph.

Courage Begins with One Voice

Before You Read

1 Previewing to Determine Organization

- Direct students' attention to the information in the Reading Tip in the margin. Explain as needed.
- Read the directions and the three patterns of organization, and explain as needed.
- Give students time to skim the article and decide which pattern is used.
- Take a vote to see which pattern was chosen by the most students.
- Give them the right answer and discuss why this is the best choice.

ANSWER KEY

2

2 Using Expressive Synonyms

- Read the directions.
- Model the activity by completing the first item as a class.
- Have students complete the rest of the activity independently.
- Go over the answers.

ANSWER KEY

1. lament
2. eloquence
3. valor
4. overwhelming
5. take up the torch
6. atrocities
7. compelling
8. sacrifice
9. monitors
10. obstacles
11. conduct
12. atone

Read

- Read the Introduction aloud or have a volunteer read it.
- Discuss the questions as a class.
- Allow students 10 minutes to read the passage.

Content Note

- Kerry Kennedy is a member of the famous American Kennedy family. Her uncle was President John F. Kennedy and her father was presidential hopeful Robert F. Kennedy. She was born September 8, 1959 and attended Brown University and Boston College Law School before marrying Andrew Cuomo, who is a member of another famous American political family. They have since separated and divorced. Kerry Kennedy founded The Robert F. Kennedy Memorial Center for Human Rights for which she led a delegation to Liberia in 1994. She currently serves on the Board of Directors for The Robert F. Kennedy Memorial.

After You Read

FOCUS

Identifying the Voices in a Reading

- Read the information in the instruction note and explain as needed.
- Tell students they can identify what words are direct quotes by the author's use of quotation marks.
- Give students 1–2 minutes to skim the reading and find an example of a direct quote.
- Call on a few students to read the quotations they found.

3 Identifying the Voices

- Read the directions, and explain as needed
- Have students complete the activity independently.
- Go over the answers.

ANSWER KEY

1. d **2.** a **3.** b **4.** e **5.** c

FOCUS

Using Noun Suffixes to Create New Words

- Read the information in the instruction note and explain as needed.
- Remind students that they should study their notes about suffixes from Chapter 6 and from Part 1 of Chapter 7.
- Ask students to think of a new word for each of the suffixes listed.
- Compile a list on the board.

4 Using Noun Suffixes to Create New Words

- Read the directions and model the activity by completing the first item as a class.
- Have students complete the rest of the activity independently.
- Go over the answers.

ANSWER KEY

1. perception
2. expression
3. commitment
4. repression
5. responsibility
6. assistance
7. negotiations
8. preparations
9. demilitarization
10. investments
11. decisions
12. servitude

5 Focusing on Words from the Academic Word List

- Read the directions and direct students' attention to the words in the vocabulary box.
- Have students complete the activity independently.
- Review correct answers as a class.
- Check comprehension by asking students to use the vocabulary words in new sentences. or phrases.

ANSWER KEY

1. assistance **2.** medical **3.** role **4.** civil
5. monitors **6.** violations **7.** Promotion
8. founded **9.** depressed **10.** energy

6 Guided Academic Conversation: How Do You Measure Courage?

Best Practice

Interacting with Others

The questions in Activity 6, Guided Academic Conversation, ask students how they measure courage. This activity gets students to engage in lively, authentic discussions, which require them to express their ideas clearly and comprehend those of other students. Interactive activities such as this help build students' confidence and fluency.

- Put students in small groups to discuss the questions.
- Once they have finished, tell them to join another group and compare their answers.

Expansion Activity

- The aim of this activity is to practice writing interview questions based on the reading passage in Part 2.
- Tell students to choose one of the human rights heroes mentioned in the reading passage.
- Tell them to imagine they are going to interview that person on a news program.
- Have them write 3-5 interview questions based on information they would like to find out about this person.
- Tell them to try to use words they have learned in this chapter in their questions.
- Put students in pairs and have them explain to their partner why they chose the person they did and share their interview questions.
- Ask volunteers to share some of the questions they wrote that use words from the chapter.
- Make a list of the questions on the board.

1 Making Connections

- Go over the topics, and explain as needed.
- Tell students to choose one of the topics and research it.
- If you have access to a computer lab, you can do this as a lab activity. If not, you can assign it for homework.
- Schedule time during the next class for students to report on their findings.

Responding in Writing

FOCUS

Writing Tip: Using a Venn Diagram to Compare and Contrast

- Read the Writing Tip.
- Model how to use a Venn diagram by drawing one on the board and asking students to compare and contrast two famous people.
- Brainstorm similarities and differences and write them in the Venn diagram on the board.

2 Comparing and Contrasting Two Leaders

- Read the directions.
- Tell students to refer back to information in the chapter to review facts about the leaders they choose to compare.
- Encourage students to work independently as they follow the steps.
- Have students draw a Venn diagram describing two leaders and continue to use their diagram as they complete the writing steps.

FOCUS ON TESTING TOEFL® iBT

Sentence-Insertion Questions on Tests

- Read the information in the Focus on Testing section, and explain as needed.
- Have students complete the Practice activity.
- Go over the answers.

ANSWER KEY

After square 3.

Self-Assessment Log

- Encourage students to maintain a self-assessment log.
- Allow class time so students can check the strategies and vocabulary they learned in the chapter.
- Tell students to find definitions in the chapter for any words they did not check.

CHAPTER 8

Creativity

In this CHAPTER

Students will read about three famous creative individuals—inventor Thomas Alva Edison, architect Zaha Hadid, and technology genius Steve Jobs. The articles offer students insight into how creativity is nurtured and expressed. Students will expand their vocabulary work on compound words, finding definitions from context and the use of pictorial language. Higher order tasks—inferencing, synthesizing, and argument—are included in the chapter.

> "Creativity comes from looking for the unexpected and stepping outside of your own experience."
>
> Masaru Ibuka
> Co-founder of Sony

Chapter Opener

- Ask students if they know these names: Thomas Alva Edison, Zaha Hadid, Steve Jobs. Have students discuss what they might have in common. (creativity)
- Direct students' attention to the photo of the statue on page 172 in the Student Book. Ask if they know its name and why it's famous. (*The Thinker*, by French sculptor Auguste Rodin, 1902.)
- Read the quotation by Masaru Ibuka (1908–1997) on page 172 and have students tell what they think it means.
- Have students create a definition of *creativity*.

Chapter Overview

Reading Selections

Pure Genius by Michael Michalko

"I Don't Do Nice" by Jonathan Glancey

Reading Skills and Strategies

Scanning for compound words

Recognizing nouns and verbs by definition and context

Inferring character from actions

Previewing an interview for organization and key ideas

Critical-Thinking Skills

Understanding the power of pictorial language

Summarizing group discussions and reporting them to the class

Synthesizing Internet content: Taking notes and presenting results

Writing Tip: Making a plan before beginning to describe an object or invention

Vocabulary Building

Matching set phrases or expressions to their content

Guessing the meaning of words from structure and context

Focusing on words from the Academic Word List

Focus on Testing TOEFL® iBT

Thinking twice about tricky test questions

Vocabulary

Nouns
- architect
- architecture
- assumptions*
- authorities*
- commissions*
- construction*
- contraption
- dedication
- deficiencies
- design*
- draftsman
- dud
- exclusives*
- experiment
- genius
- insecurity
- inspiration
- invention
- marshes
- mentor
- patents
- priority*
- quantity
- quotas
- teams*
- typewriter

Verbs
- articulate
- compress
- conduct*
- create*
- diluting
- divert
- generate*
- persist*
- publish*
- research*
- rethink
- transmitted*

Adjectives
- cavernous
- conceptual*
- contemporary*
- intelligent*
- isolated*
- major*
- imaginative
- preserved
- turbulent

Idioms and Expressions
- as springboards
- contrary to popular belief
- for sure
- in the light of
- in retrospect
- on the lookout

*These words are from the Academic Word List. For more information on this list, see www.victoria.ac.nz/lals/resources/academicwordlist/

Pure Genius

Content Notes

- Thomas Alva Edison (1847–1931) was an influential American inventor and businessman and, in fact, one of the most prolific inventors in U.S. history.
- Edison is credited with numerous inventions that impact our lives today. He expanded the distribution of electricity to streets, homes, and businesses in the early 20th century. This led to the modern industrial developments and the lifestyle we enjoy. His research influenced the telephone, telegraph, phonograph, X-ray equipment, electric trains, and light bulbs, to mention a few essentials of contemporary life.
- Edison's entrepreneurial ventures were many; he founded 14 corporations, including General Electric, a major U.S. corporation still today.
- Edison had little formal schooling and was largely self-taught.

Before You Read

1 Scanning for Compound Words

- Read the instructions aloud.
- Review scanning techniques with students. The purpose of this activity is to preview some vocabulary that will aid comprehension of the reading.
- Remind students not to read word-by-word but to just look for the vocabulary in the activity. They will have an opportunity to read the article closely later.
- You may want to have students work in pairs and then compare their answers with another pair of students and the class.

ANSWER KEY

1. cast-iron
2. notebooks
3. temperature-controlled
4. brainstorm
5. everyday (in contrast to "every day")
6. horse-drawn
7. long-lasting
8. springboard
9. hearing-impaired
10. so-called
11. deep-seated
12. cause-and-effect

Strategy

Recognizing Nouns and Verbs by Definition and Context

- Read the information in the Strategy box.
- Discuss the different meanings, parts of speech, and pronunciation of the examples.
- Have students check their English dictionary to see how stress is marked.

2 Recognizing Nouns and Verbs by Definitions and Context

- Read the directions.
- Have students complete the activity independently and then compare their answers with a partner.
- Remind students to cross off the words as they use them.

ANSWER KEY

1. patents	5. quotas	9. persist
2. assumptions	6. inspiration	10. rethink
3. generate	7. dud	11. research
4. quantity	8. conduct	12. deficiencies

Read

Best Practice

Activating Prior Knowledge

The first column in a KWL chart such as the one used in the following Expansion Activity always requires students to draw on what they already know about a topic, in this case, Thomas Edison. By recalling what they already know, students are prepared to handle new information in the reading selection.

REPRODUCIBLE Expansion Activity

- The aim of this activity is to have students organize their ideas before, during, and after the reading.
- Before students read the passage, photocopy and distribute Black Line Master "KWL Chart" on page BLM16 of this Teacher's Manual.
- Explain to the class that a KWL chart will help them remember and organize what they read. "K" stands for "What I Know." Student should write information they already know about Thomas Edison in the first column.
- Be sure that students understand that there are no wrong answers. They should write what they know or believe to be true.
- "W" stands for "What I Want to Know."Students should fill this column in with questions about the topic that they would like to learn.
- "L" stand for "What I Learned."Students should complete this column after they read the selection.
- Encourage students to use the KWL chart for textbook reading.
- Have students fill in the "K" and "W" columns before they read the article about Thomas Edison.
- Once they finish the reading, they will fill in the "L" column.
- Have students compare their charts with a partner and the class. You may want to collect and check their work.

- Have a student volunteer read the Introduction to the reading passage on page 177 in the Student Book.
- Instruct students to read silently or follow along with the audio.

After You Read

3 Matching Set Phrases or Expressions to their Context

- Read the information describing set phrases and the activity instructions.
- Review the example with the class.
- Have students complete the activity independently and then compare their answers with a partner.
- Remind students to cross off the expressions as they use them.

ANSWER KEY

1. In his mind **2.** in the light of **3.** Contrary to popular belief **4.** as springboards **5.** in retrospect **6.** on the lookout **7.** for sure

Strategy

Inferring Character from Actions

- Read the information in the Strategy box and explain as needed.

4 Inferring Character from Actions

Best Practice

Cultivating Critical Thinking

Activities such as this require students to use critical thinking skills, for example, drawing conclusions from information they read. In this case, students are drawing conclusions about Thomas Edison and his personal characteristics by inferring from the information given in the article.

- Read the directions aloud.
- Tell students to review the text to determine if the descriptions of Edison are true or false.
- Have students indicate the paragraph on which they based their answer. There may be several places in the article where the answer can be justified.
- Review the answers with the whole class and discuss any differences of opinion.

ANSWER KEY

1. false (paragraph E)
2. true (paragraph D)
3. true (paragraph I)
4. true (paragraph E)
5. false (paragraph I)
6. false (paragraph G)
7. false (no reference, inferred)
8. false (paragraph H)
9. true (paragraph E)
10. false (paragraph I)

5 Guided Academic Conversation

- Divide students into small groups to discuss the questions.
- Move around the classroom and make sure that all students are participating.
- Once the time is up, combine groups so students can compare answers.
- Discuss any questions or comments during a whole-class discussion.

6 What Do You Think?

- Have students read the paragraph "On Being Creative" on page 181 of the Student Book.
- Instruct students to write their answers the questions that follow the reading independently. Tell them to be prepared to share the information with a classmate.
- Organize students into small groups to discuss their answers to the questions.
- Compare students' answers to question 3. Is there a consensus of the favorites?
- Have students share their group members' most creative answers to questions 2 and 4.

"I Don't Do Nice"

Before You Read

1 Previewing an Interview for Organization and Key Ideas

- Assign students to work independently or with a partner.
- Read the directions aloud.
- Instruct students to make notes of their answers to the questions.
- Discuss the answers with the whole class.

ANSWER KEY

Answers will vary.

1. The person is an architect; the buildings she designs are very unusual and creative and are found around the world.
2. This is not a direct quotation but adapted from the interviewee's comment in Paragraph G, "I don't design nice buildings… ."
3. This article uses the second type of interview organization.

2 Guessing the Meaning of Words from Structure and Context

- Read the directions.
- Have students find the answers independently.
- When finished, instruct students to compare their answers with a partner. If there is disagreement, have them consult other students.
- Check answers with the whole class.

ANSWER KEY

1. D **2.** A **3.** D **4.** D **5.** B **6.** C
7. C **8.** B **9.** D **10.** C

Read

- Have a volunteer read the Introduction aloud.
- Explain that the title of the reading selection—"I Don't Do Nice"—is a quotation by the architect Zaha Hadid. This statement uses the adjective "nice" as a noun. Hadid means that she does not design nice buildings—that is, buildings that are merely okay or conventional.
- Instruct students to read silently or you may wish to play the audio as they read.
- Set an appropriate time limit (10 minutes) to encourage reading fluency.

After You Read

Strategy

Understanding the Power of Pictorial Language

- Read the information in the Strategy box.
- Bring some additional examples of similes and metaphors to share with the class.

3 Understanding the Power of Pictorial Language

- Read the directions.
- Review the first item with the class. Clarify and answer any questions.
- Have students work independently or with a partner to write the explanations of the pictorial language.
- Review the responses as a whole class activity.

ANSWER KEY

Answers will vary.

1. The room is being compared to a cave. This makes it seem big and set apart from normal life.

2. The opera house has branches stretching out into the sea, like the legs of a starfish.
3. The buildings were bright and shiny—like jewels standing out from their surroundings.
4. The image is one of a flowing, different landscape that connects modern cities and the people in them.
5. Her buildings are not refined, smoothly polished, or dull. They are alive.
6. There are so many people working with her that there is hardly room; they have to work in every space they can find, even if it's overhead.

Expansion Activity

- The aim of this Expansion Activity is to have students notice pictorial language, similes, and metaphors.
- Have students look for examples of pictorial language in advertisements, quotations, or sentences that they find in a magazine, book, or on the Internet.
- Put students into small groups to share and explain their pictorial language examples.
- Have each group select their favorite examples and present them to the whole class.

4 Focusing on Words from the Academic Word List

- Read the directions.
- Remind students to do the activity without looking back at the reading passage.
- After students finish, they can check their answers with a partner and with the reading on pages 184–186 in the Student Book.

ANSWER KEY

1. design
2. publish
3. construction
4. create
5. isolated
6. contemporary
7. major
8. teams
9. designed
10. intelligent
11. authorities

5 Guided Academic Conversation

Best Practice

Interacting with Others

This small group activity requires students to discuss the topics that were brought up in the interview with Zaha Hadid. Students share their opinions and consolidate their ideas to present to the whole class. This prepares them for the type of collaborative work they will encounter in various academic settings.

- Divide students into small groups.
- Explain that they are to share their responses with the group and come up with a consensus.
- If students cannot agree, they should find ways to present the various points of view brought up by their group members.
- Assign one person to take notes, another person to facilitate discussion, and one person to present the group's responses to the class.
- Debrief by having the spokesperson for each group report their group's discussion results.
- Be sure to set a time limit and to pace the work so that all groups finish all items in the activity.

FOCUS ON TESTING TOEFL® iBT

Thinking Twice about Tricky Questions

- Have students follow along as you read the information about tricky questions.
- Note to students that test items generally follow the order of appearance in the text, which helps them locate answers more quickly.
- Go over the first item together with students.
- Ask them for the correct answer and their reason for the choice. On what facts did they base their choice? (C, a hard worker who doesn't care what other people think, "I don't design nice buildings—I don't like them." The other response choices are not supported by the passage.
- Read the directions to the Practice section.
- Have students work with a partner and discuss why the questions are or are not tricky.
- Remind students to apply what they learned about making inferences about characters on page 180 in the Student Book.
- Ask students to share their responses with the class.

ANSWER KEY

2. D (not tricky: all of the above are listed in the interview) **3.** C (not tricky: answer is in the text **4.** B (not tricky: the other choices are all refuted in the interview) **5.** A (tricky: all the choices are true about Hadid, but only answer A is explicitly stated as a quotation) **6.** C (tricky; one could imply that the other choices are true but they are not supported by the information in the interview; C is the best answer because of the word "probably," and the architect's statement in paragraph F that "architecture requires 100% dedication")

1 Making Connections

- Read the directions.
- Review each of the four research topics with the class.
- Have students each select a topic or have them work with a partner to research jointly.
- If you have access to a computer lab, you can do this as a lab activity. Alternatively, students can work on their own.
- Remind students to document their sources.
- If equipment is available, have students create a presentation using presentation software. If students do the work without technology, have them include photos and illustrations to share.
- Schedule time in the class period for students to present their work.

Responding in Writing

FOCUS

Writing Tip: Make a Plan before Beginning to Describe an Object or Invention

- Read the information in the Focus box.
- Use some examples to demonstrate planning a description of an object, such as the Eiffel Tower, a landmark in your community, or an item you bring in to class.

2 Describing an Architectural Marvel or a Marvelous Machine

Best Practice

Scaffolding Instruction

This writing activity uses students' prior knowledge and the writing steps as scaffolds. Students will draw on what they know about a particular object or building, as well as the strategies they have learned in this chapter and earlier chapters: organizing ideas, using descriptive details, using pictorial language, etc.

- Read the directions.
- Give students the assignment to find a photo or bring a small object to class. However, they should not show it to anyone.
- Go over the Steps listed in the activity with students.
- Have students plan and write their description.
- Students can share their description with a small group.
- Select model descriptions to share with the entire class.
- When possible, display students' descriptions and photos for everyone to read.

3 Around the Globe: Steve Jobs, Another Creative Genius for the 21st Century

- Have a volunteer read the directions.
- Ask the class if they have used any of the devices created by Steve Jobs. What do they think of them?
- Instruct students to read the article silently and take notes of three or four things that they think are important or interesting as they read.
- After students finish reading, have them use their notes to share with a partner or the class.

- Read aloud the three items that follow the reading, on the bottom on page 194 in the Student Book.
- Have students work in small groups to discuss their answers to the questions.
- Ask for volunteers to share their responses with the whole class.

Expansion Activity

- The aim of this activity is to practice interaction through a topic-related debate.
- Tell students that they will participate in a friendly debate.
- Divide the class into two teams: male and female, if possible. If the class is large, you may have more teams; be certain that both sides of the question are assigned to different groups.
- Give students the debate topic: *Who is more creative, men or women?* Tell them that each team will have five minutes to present their opinion.
- Have the teams work on their response.
- Allow five minutes for each team to present their argument.
- Consider having another teacher or a third group judge the best argument.
- For a challenge, you can have the men argue that women are more creative while the women argue that men are more creative.

Self-Assessment Log

- Reinforce the advantages of a Self-Assessment Log for students to analyze their progress.
- Have them check the strategies and vocabulary that they learned.
- Suggest that they review any elements of the chapter that they do not understand. Direct them to find the place(s) in the chapter where the strategy or vocabulary is presented and practiced.
- Address any questions and review strategies and vocabulary as needed.

CHAPTER 9

Human Behavior

In this CHAPTER

Students will focus on human behavior. In the first reading, they will learn about the ways people evaluate their own culture and other cultures. Students will learn about ethnocentrism and how it can be seen in many aspects of culture—including literature and language. In Part 2, students will read a short story about how people are influenced by their environments. New vocabulary, reading strategies, and critical thinking will be brought together as students create dialogues in Part 3.

> "Let a person so act by day that he or she may rest happily by night."
>
> Japanese proverb

Chapter Opener

- Direct student's attention to the photo and have them work in small groups to discuss the questions in the **Connecting to the Topic** section.
- Call on groups to recount their discussions with the whole class.
- Read the Japanese proverb aloud and ask students what they think it means.

Chapter Overview

Reading Selections

Ethnocentrism by John Friedl

A Clean, Well-Lighted Place by Ernest Hemingway

Reading Skills and Strategies

Skimming for the main idea

Scanning for development of the main idea

Finding support for main ideas

Previewing for characters and plot

Expressing the theme

Critical-Thinking Skills

Comparing opinions

Analyzing love poems (Readings: three poems)

Making inferences about characters

Synthesizing Internet content: Taking notes and presenting results

Writing Tip: Creating a dialogue

Vocabulary Building

Using prefixes to build new words

Scanning for words with clues

Focusing on words from the Academic Word List

Getting the meaning of words from context

Focus on Testing TOEFL® iBT

Answering questions on tests about an author's purposes or attitudes

(Reading: *Gestural Ethnocentrism*)

Vocabulary

Nouns

- aspect*
- barbarian
- bias*
- colleague*
- culture*
- despair
- ethnocentrism
- hue
- insomnia
- omission of syntax
- outcome*
- outlook
- self-evaluation
- subgroup
- world view

Adjectives

- aware*
- distasteful
- inconceivable*
- inhuman
- irrational*
- liberal*
- non-Western
- open-minded
- repugnant
- repulsive
- sexual*
- subarctic
- unnatural

Adverbs

- constantly*
- objectively*

*These words are from the Academic Word List. For more information on this list, see www.victoria.ac.nz/lals/resources/academicwordlist/

Ethnocentrism

Before You Read

- Go over the information in the Reading Tip in the margin, and explain as needed.
- Ask students to guess the meaning of "ethnocentrism."

1 Skimming for the Main Idea

- Read the directions, and explain as needed.
- Ask students to write the author's explanation of ethnocentrism.
- Discuss the answers as a class.

ANSWER KEY

Possible answers: Ethnocentrism is the belief that one's own patterns of behavior are the best, the most natural, beautiful, right, or important. Therefore, other people who live differently live by standards that are inhuman, irrational, unnatural, or wrong. / Ethnocentrism is the view that one's own culture is better than all others; it is the way all people feel about themselves as compared to outsiders.

2 Scanning for the Development of the Main Idea

- Read the directions, and explain as needed.
- Have students complete the activity on their own.
- Discuss the answers as a class.

ANSWER KEY

1. 5

2. ____ choice of clothing
  ✓ food preferences
  ✓ language
  ____ marriage ceremonies
  ✓ myths and folktales

3 Using Prefixes to Build New Words

- Read the directions, and explain as needed.
- Model the activity by doing item 1 as a class. Make sure students understand how the word was formed.
- Ask students to complete the activity.
- Discuss the answers as a class.
- Check comprehension by having students write sentences using the words.

ANSWER KEY

1. subartic **2.** inconceivable **3.** subgroups
4. inhuman **5.** unnatural **6.** irrational
7. distasteful **8.** non-Western

Read

- Read the Introduction aloud, or ask a volunteer to read it.
- Discuss the questions as a class.
- Have students read the passage silently within a time limit (10 minutes).

Content Note

- According to the U.S. Census Bureau, the state of Alaska has 626,932 Alaskan natives who comprise approximately 6% of the state's population.

After You Read

4 Scanning for Words with Clues

- Model the activity by reading the first definition "the way one looks at the world" and asking students to scan the reading to find it in context.
- Make sure students understand why "outlook" is the correct answer.
- Have students complete the activity individually or in pairs.
- Discuss the answers as a class.

ANSWER KEY

1. outlook, world view **2.** liberal, open-minded

3. bias **4.** self-evaluation

5. repulsive, repugnant **6.** barbarian

7. hue **8.** inconceivable

5 The Support Game: Finding Support for Main Ideas

- Put students in small teams of three to five.
- Read the directions and set a time limit of 10 minutes for students to complete the task.
- Have students report their findings.
- Have the class vote on which team is the winner.

ANSWER KEY

Possible answers:

1. In many languages, especially those of non-Western societies, the words used to refer to one's own tribe is "mankind" or "human."

   The word *Eskimo* used by the Inuit means "eaters of raw flesh"

   Inuit means "real people."

   The word *barbarian* was used to describe tribes that lived around the edge of ancient Greek society.
2. An example of ethnocentrism can be found in the myths and folktales. For example, the creation myth of the Cherokee Indians.
3. In Southeast Asia, adults do not drink milk. To Americans, it is inconceivable that people in other parts of the world do not drink milk., In China, dog meat is a delicacy; but would make most Americans feel sick. Horse meat is also rejected by most Americans. The attitude of Indians toward eating beef is similar to the views of Americans about eating dogs. The attitude of Chinese people towards eating dogs is similar to Americans' attitudes toward cows.

6 Focusing on Words from the Academic Word List

- Read the directions, and explain as necessary.
- Tell students to complete this activity on their own.
- Review the correct answers as a class.
- Check comprehension by asking students to use words in new sentences.

ANSWER KEY

1. culture **2.** liberal **3.** aspect **4.** culture

5. sexual **6.** outcome **7.** constantly **8.** aware

9. objectively **10.** bias

7 Guided Academic Conversation

- Put students in small groups to discuss the topics.
- Move around the classroom to ensure that students are participating.
- Combine groups to share opinions.

Best Practice

Organizing Information

A Venn diagram is a visual tool that can help students make connections and see relationships between two things. It can also help them remember information through visual cues. Teachers can use Venn diagrams to assess students' understanding of the material and their ability to categorize information. The Venn diagram in the following Expansion Activity has students compare different types of gestures.

REPRODUCIBLE

Expansion Activity

- The purpose of this activity is to research, compare, and contrast two different cultures.
- Tell students to reflect on some of the topics covered in the reading passage, *Ethnocentrism*, and their discussions in Activity 7 on page 203. Ask them to choose a topic such as food, marriage customs, communication (gestures, greetings, language, etc.) and compare the attitudes and norms for that topic in two different cultures.
- Copy and hand out Black Line Master **Venn Diagram: Cultural Comparisons** (BLM 18).
- Model a Venn diagram on the board, and explain how it is helpful when comparing and contrasting two topics.
- Give students time to do research on the Internet or at the library. Tell them that they can also conduct their research by interviewing people from the cultures they are comparing.
- Have students complete the Venn diagrams and discuss the two questions on the BLM with a partner.
- Ask volunteers to present their findings to the entire class.

FOCUS ON TESTING TOEFL® iBT

Questions About an Author's Purposes or Attitudes

- Read the information in the Focus on Testing section, and explain as needed.
- Have students complete the practice section.
- Discuss the answers as a class.

ANSWER KEY

1. D **2.** C **3.** A **4.** B **5.** A

8 Around the Globe

Best Practice

Making Use of Academic Content

In this activity, students are reading and analyzing short love poems from different cultures. Because poetry is an integral part of secondary and university literature and English courses as well as other humanities classes, this activity will provide practice with the type of material and tasks students may encounter in other courses.

Content Notes

- **Li Po** (701–762 CE) was a native of Sichuan China. As a teenager he went to live in the mountains with a religious leader named Tunyen-tzu. He later left and became a wandering poet. He wrote many poems during his lifetime, primarily about solitude, friendship, the passage of time, and nature. He is recognized as one of the greatest Tang poets.

  Source: www.humanisticletexts.org

- **Ono no Kamachi** lived during the mid-800s in Japan, was born into a literary family, and was perhaps an attendant to Emperor Nimmei. Other than this, little else is known about her. Most of her poems are about love and the melancholy surrounding it.

  Source: home.infoonline.net

- **Hafiz** lived sometime around 1310–1325 CE in south-central Iran. His real name was Shamseddin Mohammed, but his pen name was Hafiz or Hafez, which means one who has memorized the Koran. His poetry is written in Ghazal form, which is a strict Persian form of poetry comparable to English sonnets. Although there have been many attempts to translate his poetry into English, it is said that even the best translations are not fully successful.

  Source: hafizonlove.com

- Put students in groups of three to five. Ask them to read the poems aloud in their groups and answer the questions that follow.
- Call on students to share their group's answers and opinions.

A Clean, Well-Lighted Place

Before You Read

1 Previewing for Characters and Plot

- Read the information about Ernest Hemingway.
- Read the instructions, and have students find the answer the questions.
- Go over the answers.

ANSWER KEY

1. three
2. dialogue
3. sad; Answers may include: The young waiter is unhappy about working late; The old man is in despair and lonely.

2 Getting the Meaning of Words from Context

- Read the directions, and model the activity by doing the first item as a class.
- Have students complete the activity independently.
- Go over the answers.

ANSWER KEY

1. B **2.** C **3.** A **4.** B **5.** A **6.** C

Read

- Read or have a volunteer read the Introduction aloud.
- Discuss the questions as a class.
- Give students 10–15 minutes to read the story.

Content Note

- In the year 2010, there were an estimated 40 million Americans aged 65 or older. Approximately 14% of those older American men had been widowed (their wives had died). Over 44% of women had lost their husbands. Those widows and widowers are more depressed and lonely than other age groups who still have their spouses.

Vocabulary Note

- Often in English writing, authors use words from other languages. Hemingway uses some Spanish words, and their meanings are evident from the context. Sometimes words are *cognates*, which means they are spelled similarly in both languages and mean essentially the same thing. For example, *atender* in Spanish means *to attend to* in English. Students can often determine meanings from the spelling of foreign words. Explain that although foreign words might be frustrating, they can figure out the meanings with relatively little trouble.

After You Read

3 Making Inferences about Characters

Best Practice

Cultivating Critical Thinking
In this activity students must use the information from the dialogs to make inferences about the characters in the story. This activity requires students to draw conclusions based on the information provided by the author. Making inferences is a skill that students will need to use a variety of academic contexts.

- Read the directions, and discuss the words *maybe, perhaps, probably, must.*
- Have students complete the activity.
- Go over the answers.

ANSWER KEY

Possible answers:

1. The old man must be very sad about something. He has problems. He is probably lonely or worried about his life.
2. The waiter who spoke last probably has money problems of his own, so he might think everyone is worried about money.
3. The younger waiter is probably only saying this because he is tired and wants to go home. He thinks that if the man had killed himself, he would be able to close the restaurant and go home early.
4. The older waiter probably doesn't mind staying late. Perhaps he doesn't have anyone waiting for him at home. Maybe he is as lonely as the old man.
5. The older waiter must substitute *nada* for other important words because he thinks that life for the old man and for himself is meaningless and offers them nothing, or *nada.*

Strategy

Expressing the Theme

- Read the information in the Strategy Box, and explain as needed.
- Remind students of the reading in Part 1 about human behavior (pages 199–201).
- Ask students for synonyms for "theme." Answers may include *subject* or *topic.*

4 Expressing the Theme

- Read the directions, and have students choose which statement they feel best expresses the theme.
- Ask them to think about why their choice is better than the other two.
- Put students in pairs or small groups, and have them write their own themes.
- Call on students to share their themes with the class.

ANSWER KEY

2

REPRODUCIBLE

Expansion Activity

- The aim of this activity is to have students practice making story maps.
- Copy and hand out Black Line Master **Story Map** (BLM 19).
- Explain to students that "mapping" the story will help them remember characters, events, and themes from the short story.
- Have students complete the story map for "A Clean, Well-Lighted Place" by Ernest Hemingway.
- Have them compare their story map with a partner.
- Go over the answers as a class.

5 Guided Academic Conversation

- Put students in small groups to discuss the topics.
- Have students share their opinions with the class.

6 What Do You Think?

Best Practice

Activating Prior Knowledge

By focusing on manners in the 21st century, students are able to bridge prior knowledge of the topic to material they read in the chapter. In this case, students are discussing their opinions of manners, culture, and society with which they are already familiar.

- Read the paragraph aloud, or ask a volunteer to read it.
- Put students into small groups to discuss the questions.
- Have one representative from each group share their answers.

1 Making Connections

Best Practice

Scaffolding Instruction
Activities such as this will enable students to link knowledge recently acquired in this chapter with new information that they gather from their research. In this case, students are asked to research different attitudes toward either clothing styles or the importance of Hemingway.

- Read the directions and topics aloud, and explain as needed.
- Tell students to research the topic of their choice on the Internet.
- Have students present their findings to the class.

Responding in Writing

FOCUS

Writing Tip: Creating a Dialogue

- Read the Writing Tip, and explain as needed.
- Remind students about the short story in Part 2, which contains a lot of dialogue. If you haven't done so already, you may want to take this opportunity to teach students about quotation marks. See the following Grammar Notes.

Grammar Notes

- Quotation marks are used to indicate a person's exact words. *He said, "I am going to the restaurant."*
- When a quote is broken, a comma is used before the second part of the quotation. "*I am going to the restaurant*," he said, "*but if you want to come too, that would be fine.*"
- Punctuation that ends a quotation, such as commas, periods, question marks, or exclamation points, are placed inside the quotation marks. *She shouted, "No!"*
- For dialogues, every time the speaker changes, a new paragraph needs to be started.

  He said, "Do you want to come with me?"

  "No, I have to go to school," she said.

2 Writing a Dialogue

Best Practice

Interacting with Others
Having students work with a partner to write a creative dialogue offers the chance for them to interact on two levels. First, they work together to discuss what their dialogues should be about. Second, they will read their dialogues in an attempt to make it as authentic as possible.

- Go over the directions and steps for the activity.
- Put students in pairs, and have them follow the steps.
- Move about the room and offer help to students as they write.
- Combine pairs so students can read their dialogues and get feedback.
- Collect dialogues after students have made their revisions.

Self-Assessment Log

- Encourage students to maintain a self-assessment log.
- Allow class time so students can check the strategies and vocabulary they learned in the chapter.
- Tell students to find definitions in the chapter for any words they did not check.

CHAPTER 10

Crime and Punishment

In this CHAPTER

Students will explore what causes people to commit crimes, if criminals can be reformed, and discuss what the appropriate punishments for crimes should be. In Part 1, they will read a magazine article about criminals who try to overcome their crime addiction through meetings and spiritual help. In Part 2, students will read a fictional selection, a murder mystery, with a surprise ending. New vocabulary, reading strategies, and research will be brought together as students formulate their own viewpoints in Part 3.

"The way of justice is mysterious."

Sanskrit proverb

Chapter Opener

- Direct students' attention to the photo and ask questions. *Who are the people in the photos? What's the situation?*
- Put students in small groups to discuss the questions in the **Connecting to the Topic** section. (The images show a woman being mugged by two men on a city walkway.)
- Call on groups to recount their discussions with the whole class. Compile a master list on the board.
- Read the Sanskrit proverb aloud and ask students what they think it means.

Chapter Overview

Reading Selections

Hooked on Crime by Ken MacQueen

Eye Witness by Ed McBain

Reading Skills and Strategies

Identifying the interviewees in an article

Understanding the setting

Identifying narrative elements

Scanning for specific terms

Reading and interpreting charts

Critical-Thinking Skills

Reporting opinions

Using a graphic organizer (storyboard) to summarize the plot

Interpreting a scene from the plot in a group skit

Synthesizing Internet content: Taking notes and presenting results

Writing Tip: Using a summary of an event to connect to a personal viewpoint

Vocabulary Building

Getting the meaning of specialized terms from context

Inferring the meaning of adjectives from context and structure

Focusing on words from the Academic Word List

Identifying spelling variations

Matching descriptive adjectives to their contexts

Focus on Testing TOEFL® iBT

Understanding prose summaries on tests

(Reading: *Privatized Prisons*)

Vocabulary

Nouns

- accessory
- assault
- chapter* (of an organization)
- cons
- dependency
- extortion
- fear
- heroin
- homelessness
- principles*
- robberies
- taxpayer
- tic
- tradition*
- trafficking
- underlings

Verbs

- addled
- backslide
- created*
- credits*
- deliberated
- draft*
- imposed*
- responds*

Adjectives

- burly
- clean (in the sense of "free from drugs")
- clean-cut
- contentious
- hard-luck
- jailhouse hard
- meaty
- modest
- wrenching

Adverbs

- abruptly
- carefully
- nervously
- personally
- quickly
- suspiciously
- warily
- wearily

Idioms and Expressions

- back when things were flush
- I did my time (to do time)
- making amends (make amends)
- the Old Man

*These words are from the Academic Word List. For more information on this list, see www.victoria.ac.nz/lals/resources/academicwordlist/

Hooked on Crime

Before You Read

Strategy

Identifying the Interviewees in an Article

- Read the information in the Strategy Box, and explain as needed.
- Ask students to scan the article and find the name "Stan Mingo." Explain that he is an interviewee or main character in the reading.

1 Scanning: Identifying the Interviewees

- Read the directions to the class, and explain as needed.
- Ask students to find Stan Mingo's name again and the description provided.
- Have students complete the activity independently.
- Discuss the answers as a class.

ANSWER KEY

Possible answers: **1.** Stan Mingo: a man with a "crime addiction" who is starting the meeting **2.** Gary Johnson, executive director of Harbour Light, who believes crime is addictive **3.** Rick A.: spokesman for AA who has asked that his surname not be used and who believes that spiritual principles of AA may be adopted by other addictions. **4.** Benedikt Fischer: associate professor of criminology and public health at the University of Toronto; research scientist with the Toronto-based Centre for Addiction and Mental Health, who believes that the term addiction is not "terribly helpful." **5.** George: has stolen money from family members. **6.** Rick B.: a crime and drug addict, who is feeling shame and guilt for the first time in years.

Expansion Activity

- The aim of this activity is to practice topic-related interviews.
- Tell students to imagine that they are writing an article for a newspaper and have the opportunity to interview one of the interviewees summarized in Activity 1.
- Ask students to think of good interviewing questions. Give some examples on the board such as *What is crime addiction? Do you believe a person can be addicted to crime? Why or why not? Why did you commit the crime?*
- Tell students to pick one of the interviewees and create a list of three questions they would like to ask that person.
- Consider expanding this activity by having students create a dialogue with answers from their interviewee. Answers can be developed from what students infer from the reading.

2 Getting the Meaning of Specialized Terms from Context

- Read the directions to the class.
- Model the activity by doing item 1 as a class.
- Ask students to complete the activity independently.
- Discuss the answers as a class.
- Check comprehension by having students write new sentences using the words.

ANSWER KEY

1. g **2.** m **3.** j **4.** o **5.** a **6.** d **7.** l **8.** e **9.** h **10.** f **11.** n **12.** i **13.** k **14.** c **15.** b

Vocabulary Note

- Specialized crime and drug terms are used in academic courses such as sociology, health, criminology, and criminal justice. These words are also common in the everyday language of current events. Students will see this kind of terminology in journals, magazines, and newspapers.

Read

Best Practice

Activating Prior Knowledge
Pre-reading questions, such as the ones in the Introduction to the article get students to draw upon the information they already know about the topic of crime addiction and share it with their classmates. By doing this, they will be better prepared to deal with the information presented in the article and throughout the chapter.

- Read the Introduction, or ask a student to read it aloud.
- Discuss the questions as a class.
- Have students read the passage silently within a time limit (10-15 minutes).

Content Note

- AA stands for Alcoholics Anonymous. It is an organization of people who all suffer from alcohol addiction and share their experiences, hope, and support with each other. AA is free and aims to help people stop drinking. AA has established 12 steps to overcoming an alcohol addiction. The 12 steps have been adopted by other groups formed to help people overcome other kinds of addictions, such as drug addiction and gambling addiction.

After You Read

Strategy

Understanding the Setting

- Read the information in the Strategy Box, and explain as needed.
- Ask students to tell something about the setting of the reading in Part 1.

3 Understanding the Setting

- Read the directions, and explain as needed.
- Have students complete the activity independently.
- Go over the answers.

ANSWER KEY

Possible answers: 1. alcohol, not revealed
2. 12, crime, unknown not revealed
3. alibi, heroin **4.** addiction, it guides people to safety, someone who has washed up on shore

4 Guessing the Meaning of Adjectives from Context and Structure

- Read the directions, and explain as needed.
- Have students complete the activity independently.
- Go over the answers.

ANSWER KEY

1. B **2.** A **3.** B **4.** C **5.** A **6.** C

Expansion Activity

- The aim of this activity is to provide additional practice with new vocabulary words.
- Tell students they will write a vocabulary quiz for the class.
- Have students choose three words from Activities 2 (pages 222–223) and 4 (page 228).
- Ask them to write three sentences (one for each selected word) using the words in context. Ask them to make sure the context adequately conveys the word's meaning.
- Each student should write one of their sentences on the board and draw a line where the vocabulary word should go.
- Have students copy the sentences from the board and fill in the blanks. They should be able to choose the correct vocabulary word based on the context of the sentence.

5 Focusing on Words from the Academic Word List

- Read the directions, and explain as needed.
- Tell students to complete this activity on their own.
- Tell students to check their answers on page 225.
- Go over the answers as a class.
- Check comprehension by asking students to use words in new sentences.

ANSWER KEY

1. credits 2. draft 3. chapter 4. created
5. imposed 6. responds 7. principles
8. tradition 9. principles

FOCUS

Identifying Spelling Variations

- Read the information in the instruction note, and explain as needed.
- Ask students to find examples of Canadian spelling in the reading.
- Compile a list on the board and write the American English spelling next to the Canadian spelling of the words.

6 Identifying Spelling Variations

- Read the directions.
- Have students complete the activity.
- Go over the answers.

ANSWER KEY

1. centre
2. Harbour
3. humour
4. neighbourhood

7 Guided Academic Conversation

Best Practice

Interacting with Others

Small-group discussions give students the chance to participate in authentic conversations about academic and general interest topics. Focused topics such as the questions in Activity 7 give students an opportunity to increase their fluency by expressing their ideas and opinions in conversations on a specific topic.

- Put students in small groups to read and discuss the questions.
- Ask them to discuss five of the six questions.
- Tell students that they should be prepared to report their group's opinions to the class.

8 What Do You Think?

Content Notes

- Murder is a crime that is punishable by the death penalty in some states in the U.S.
- The death penalty has been used in the United States since colonial times (the early 1800s).
- The United States is one of approximately 90 countries that enforces the death penalty.
- Although the electric chair and lethal injection are the methods used almost exclusively in the U.S., there are a few states that still maintain the firing squad, hanging, and the gas chamber as methods of execution in addition to lethal injections and/or the electric chair.
- The death penalty can be traced to Egypt in the 16th century B.C.E.

Sources: http://www.deathpenaltyinfo.org/article.php?scid=8&did=245

- Read or ask a volunteer to read the paragraph aloud.
- Put students into small groups to discuss the questions that follow.
- Have one representative from each group share answers.

Best Practice

Cultivating Critical Thinking

The following Expansion Activity will encourage critical thinking, decision making and group interaction. In this case, students must work together to develop a ranking system and support the reasons why they chose the punishments they did for each crime. By working in groups, they will need to listen to each other's ideas, be open to new opinions, and practice articulating their own ideas.

REPRODUCIBLE

Expansion Activity

- The purpose of this activity is to have students practice ranking crimes on a continuum, and doing topic-related Internet research.
- Copy and hand out Black Line Master **Ranking the Crimes** (BLM 20).
- Have students brainstorm the names of crimes. You may want to have them brainstorm crimes according to certain categories, i.e. violent crimes, such as murder and assault, crimes that involve stealing, such as shoplifting, pick pocketing, etc.
- Write a list of the crimes on the board.
- Put students in small groups.
- Have students choose ten crimes from the list on the board or any other crimes they can think of. When they have their lists, have them rank them on the continuum from "most serious" to "least serious" and then think of an appropriate punishment or sentence for each crime.
- Give students time to do research on the Internet or in the school library if necessary.
- Have students complete the continuum.
- Call on students to present their work to the class.

Eye Witness

Before You Read

1 Identifying Narrative Elements

- Read the directions, and explain as needed.
- Remind students that the three elements of a story are setting, characters, and plot.
- Have students complete the activity independently.
- Go over the answers.

ANSWER KEY

Possible answers: 1. The title tells us that the main character witnessed a murder. His eyes are brown, he doesn't smile, his mouth is thin, and he has a tic over his left cheekbone. He is nervous. He is thin and has a moustache. He dresses neatly. His name is Mr. Struthers and he is important because he witnessed a crime. He only wants to speak to the lieutenant. **2.** The narrator is the police officer who is interviewing Mr. Struthers. He is not an omniscient narrator. His name is Detective Cappeli. **3.** Magruder is a police officer who had served on the force for a long time. **4.** The victim is Lieutenant Anderson's wife. She was mugged and stabbed.

2 Scanning for Specific Terms

- Read the directions and explain as needed.
- Model the activity by doing the first item as a class.
- Have students complete the activity.
- Go over the answers.
- Check comprehension by having students use the words in new sentences.

ANSWER KEY

1. tic **2.** underlings **3.** taxpayer
4. Old Man **5.** fear **6.** accessory
7. deliberated

Read

- Read the Introduction aloud, or ask a volunteer to read it.
- Tell students to read the passage. Set a time limit (10–15 minutes).

Content Notes

- Edgar Allen Poe, an American author, is credited with writing the first mystery novel. Poe lived in the early 1800s. In 1841, he wrote *The Murders in the Rue Morgue*. The story's plot revolves around Chevalier C. Auguste Dupin who solves the crime and appears in several other Poe stories.
- One of the more famous mystery detectives is Sherlock Holmes. His character was created by Sir Arthur Conan Doyle.
- A real-life mystery is the story of the Boston Strangler. Albert Henry DeSalvo terrorized Boston from 1962–1964. He committed 13 murders before he was captured and sentenced to life in prison. He was murdered himself six years into his prison term. Even now, there are people who believe DeSalvo did not commit the crimes and the real Boston Strangler escaped punishment.

After You Read

Expansion Activity

REPRODUCIBLE

- The aim of this activity it to practice organizing the elements of the story "Eye Witness" using a chart.
- Copy and hand out Black Line Master **Story Elements Chart** ("Eye Witness") (BLM 21).
- Explain that this is a good way to organize details from the story.
- Ask students to fill in the story elements.
- Compare answers.

3 Finding Descriptive Adverbs

- Read the directions, and explain as needed. Remind students that adverbs are used to describe verbs.
- Have students complete the activity independently.
- Go over the answers.

ANSWER KEY

1. nervously	**5.** suspiciously
2. carefully	**6.** abruptly
3. personally	**7.** quickly
4. warily	**8.** wearily

Grammar Notes

- Most adverbs end with the suffix *-ly*. Some adverbs require no suffix: *least, worst, well, much,* and *little*. Adverbs can be categorized into four general groups:
- Adverbs of degree (describe the extent): Examples include *more*, *very*, *barely*.
- Adverbs of time (describe when): Examples include *then*, *soon*, *now*.
- Adverbs of place (describe where): Examples include *here*, *nowhere*, *there*.
- Adverbs of manner (describe how): Examples include *quickly*, *happily* and all of the examples from Activity 3.

Strategy

Understanding the Plot

- Read the information in the Strategy Box, and explain as needed.
- Walk students through the main events of the mystery, and have them identify which parts are significant to the plot.

Expansion Activity

REPRODUCIBLE

- The aim of this activity is to provide practice with sequencing the events of a story using a story sequencing map.
- Copy and hand out Black Line Master **Story Sequence Map** (BLM 22).
- Explain that a story sequence map is an excellent way to organize the details and plot from a story.
- Have them fill in the conflict, complications, climax, and ending of "Eye Witness" as defined in the Strategy Box.
- After they have completed their maps, put students in pairs or small groups to compare maps.
- Go over the answers.

4 Making a Storyboard of "Eye Witness" for TV

Best Practice

Organizing Information

A storyboard is a sequential depiction of a story. A storyboard will help students recall the key parts of the narrative and pull the most important details from the story. The visual nature of this activity will help students remember the most important events of the story, and the order in which they occurred.

- Put students in pairs.
- Read the directions and steps, and explain as needed.

5 You Are on TV!

- Put students in small groups and read the directions.
- Have students prepare to perform their storyboard.
- Tell each group to choose a director and actors for each character.
- Have each group act out their storyboard for the class.

Expansion Activity

- The aim of this activity is to practice interactions through a fun theme-related group activity.
- Consider a variation of Activity 5 (page 239).
- Have all the groups act out their storyboards.
- Have students vote for winners in Academy Awards categories such as Best Performance, Best Actor, Best Actress, Best Director, Best Supporting Actor.
- Collect the votes and put the winning names into envelopes.
- Stage an Academy Awards show and have student presenters read the nominees and pull the winning name from the envelope and announce the winners.

6 Guided Academic Conversation

- Put students in small groups to discuss the topics.
- Compare answers as a class.

FOCUS ON TESTING TOEFL® iBT

Prose Summaries on Tests

- Read the information in the Focus on Testing section, and explain as needed.
- Have students complete the practice.
- Go over the answer.

ANSWER KEY

a, d, e

1 Interpreting Charts

- Go over the directions.
- Have students read the information in the box about the U.S. Prison Population.
- Put students in pairs to complete the activity.
- Go over the answers.
- Allow time for students to answer the discussion questions.
- Have pairs share their answers with the class.

ANSWER KEY

1. 9 **2.** Up **3.** Federal

2 Making Connections

Best Practice

Scaffolding Instruction
Activities such as this will enable students to link knowledge recently acquired with new information they gather from their research.

- Read the directions and research topics aloud.
- Tell students to research the topic of their choice on the Internet.
- Have students report on their findings to the class.

Responding in Writing

FOCUS

Writing Tip: Developing Your Viewpoint

- Read the Writing Tip and explain as needed.
- Ask students to share their viewpoint on a topic covered in the chapter.

3 Writing About a Real Crime

Best Practice

Making Use of Academic Content
By reading an article and following the steps outlined in this activity, students will learn to how to write well-organized compositions about an article they have read. The skills they learn by doing this activity can be applied to the types of tasks they may be required to do in a broad range of academic settings.

- Read the directions and steps, and have students choose a topic.
- Have students work individually.
- Draw a sample cluster diagram on the board. Remind them to refer back to Chapter 6.
- Move about the room and offer suggestions as students write.
- Collect articles, cluster diagrams, outlines, and compositions after students have made their revisions.

Self-Assessment Log

- Encourage students to maintain a self-assessment log.
- Allow class time so students can check the strategies and vocabulary they learned in the chapter.
- Tell students to find definitions in the chapter for any words they did not check.

Chapter 1 Part 1: Compound Words

DIRECTIONS: Match each of the words in column 1 with a word in column 2 to create a compound word. When you have finished matching all of the words, create new words using each part of the compound words and write them at the bottom of the page. When you finish, share your findings with the rest of the class.

Column 1:	Column 2:
1. bed	**A.** ship
2. black	**B.** chair
3. friend	**C.** room
4. sweet	**D.** light
5. basket	**E.** watch
6. mail	**F.** box
7. wild	**G.** life
8. wrist	**H.** ball
9. arm	**I.** berry
10. sun	**J.** heart

New Words

*bed*bug, bath*room*

Name ______________________ Date ______________ REPRODUCIBLE BLM 2

Chapter 1 Part 2: Comparing Two Countries Venn Diagram

DIRECTIONS: Think about a country you know. Think about the differences and similarities between that country and the United States.

1. Label one circle in the Venn diagram with the name of the country you picked. Put things that describe that country in the left side of the circle.
2. In the other circle, put things that describe the U.S.
3. In the middle, where the circles overlap, put things that are the same in both countries.

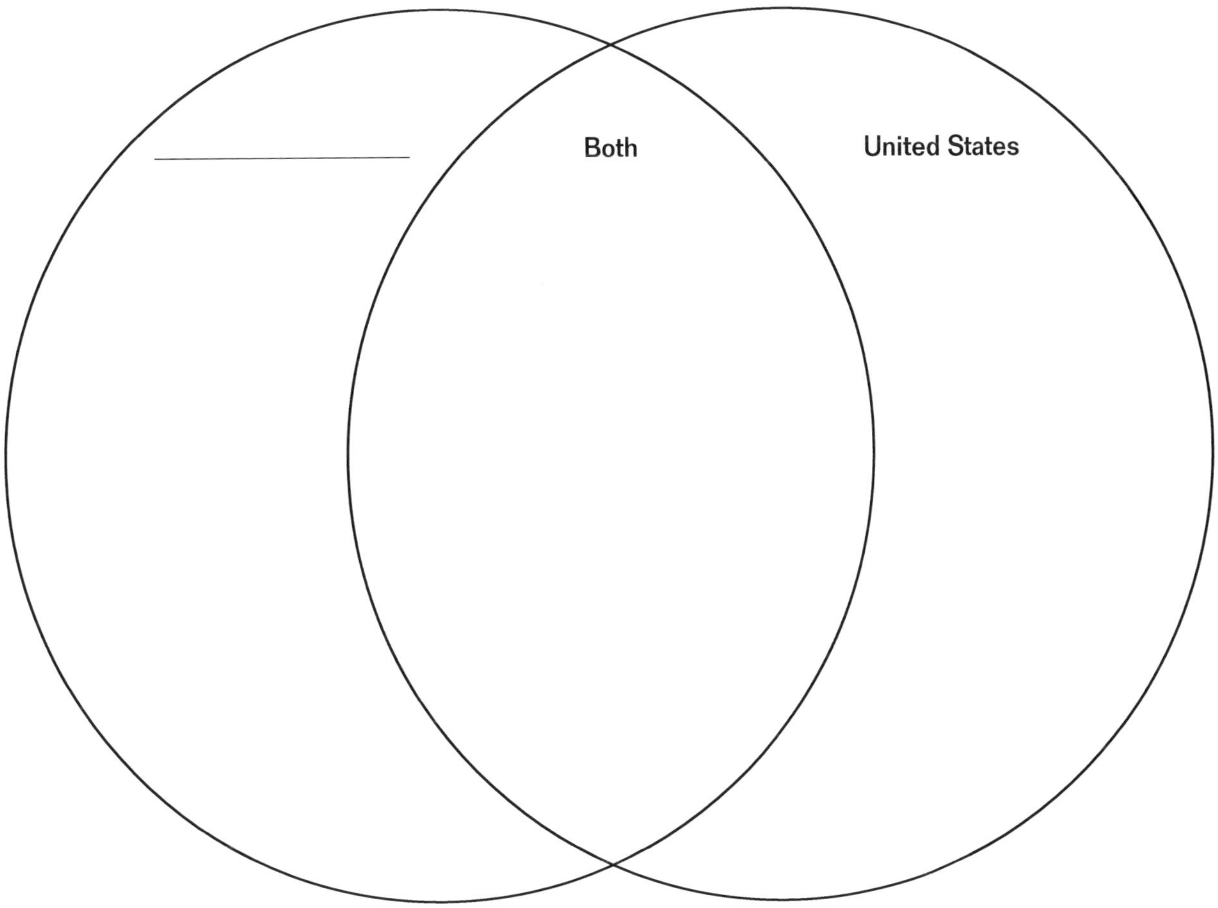

Name ______________________ Date ______________ REPRODUCIBLE BLM 3

Chapter 2 Part 1: Idiom Puzzles

Idioms from "Beckham: An Autobiography"

took	a	knock	or	two		
in	a	comfort	zone			
whisked	off					
didn't	really	have	a	clue		
bracing	myself					
twist	in	the	pit	of	my	stomach
get	the	drift				
be	our	night				
feel	at	home				

Idioms related to baseball

get	to	first	base	
be	off	base		
strike	out			
play	ball			
throw	a	curve	ball	
play	hard	ball		
make	a	ballpark	estimate	
hit	the	home	stretch	
two	strikes	against	him	
step	up	to	the	plate

Chapter 2 Part 1: Chain of Events Diagram: A Selection from My Autobiography

DIRECTIONS: Think of a significant time in your life. For example when you got married, moved to a new country or city, etc. Think of four events that occurred during that time. Write them in the correct sequence in the diagram below. Then explain your diagram to your partner.

First Event

↓

↓

↓

Last Event

Name ______________________ Date ______________ REPRODUCIBLE BLM 5

Chapter 2 Part 3: Competition / Teamwork T-Chart

DIRECTIONS: Complete the T-chart with your group. Write the reasons why you think competition or teamwork should be supported according to which topic you chose. Then write the reasons why the other concept should NOT be supported.

Topic: ______________________________

Competition	Teamwork

Name ______________________ Date ______________ REPRODUCIBLE BLM 6

Chapter 3 Part 2: Working With Prefixes and Suffixes

DIRECTIONS: Add a prefix or suffix, as appropriate, to the vocabulary words below. Choose from the prefixes and suffixes in the box. Some prefixes and suffixes will be used more than once. Some of the words listed have more than one possible prefix or suffix. Write the new words on the lines next to the words. Then write a sentence with the new word.

-ance	-al	-ing	-er	dis-
-ion(s)	-ent	-ness	-ive	un-

1. obsess ______________ ______________________________
2. satisfaction ______________ ______________________________
3. convention ______________ ______________________________
4. groom ______________ ______________________________
5. attract ______________ ______________________________
6. possess ______________ ______________________________
7. appear ______________ ______________________________
8. changing ______________ ______________________________
9. similar ______________ ______________________________
10. depend ______________ ______________________________
11. correspond ______________ ______________________________
12. research ______________ ______________________________
13. proportionate ______________ ______________________________
14. draw ______________ ______________________________
15. pleasant ______________ ______________________________

Name ______________________ Date ______________ REPRODUCIBLE BLM 7

Chapter 4 Part 2: Fact and Opinion Organizer

DIRECTIONS: Read your assigned paragraph and complete the Fact and Opinion Organizer. Compare your answers with the other students in your group.

Paragraph Letter ______

	Sentences from the reading Write specific sentences from the reading. Use exact wording.	**I know this is a Fact (or opinion) because...** Explain how you know that the sentence is a fact or opinion. Give signal words or other details.
FACTS Facts are statements that can be proven. You can usually find facts in other sources.		
OPINIONS Opinions are statements that express what a person thinks. They do not have evidence that you can find in another source.		

Name ______________________ Date ______________ REPRODUCIBLE BLM 8

Chapter 4 Part 2: Venn Diagram: Comparing Travel Experiences

DIRECTIONS: Discuss the following questions about the places you visited and make notes in the Venn diagram below.

1. Describe the place you visited.
2. Were there many tourists visiting? If so, describe them.
3. What was the general attitude of the locals toward the tourists?
4. How did the tourists treat the locals?
5. Do you feel the impact of tourism on that place was positive or negative? Explain.

Place I visited: ______________ **Place my partner visited:** ______________

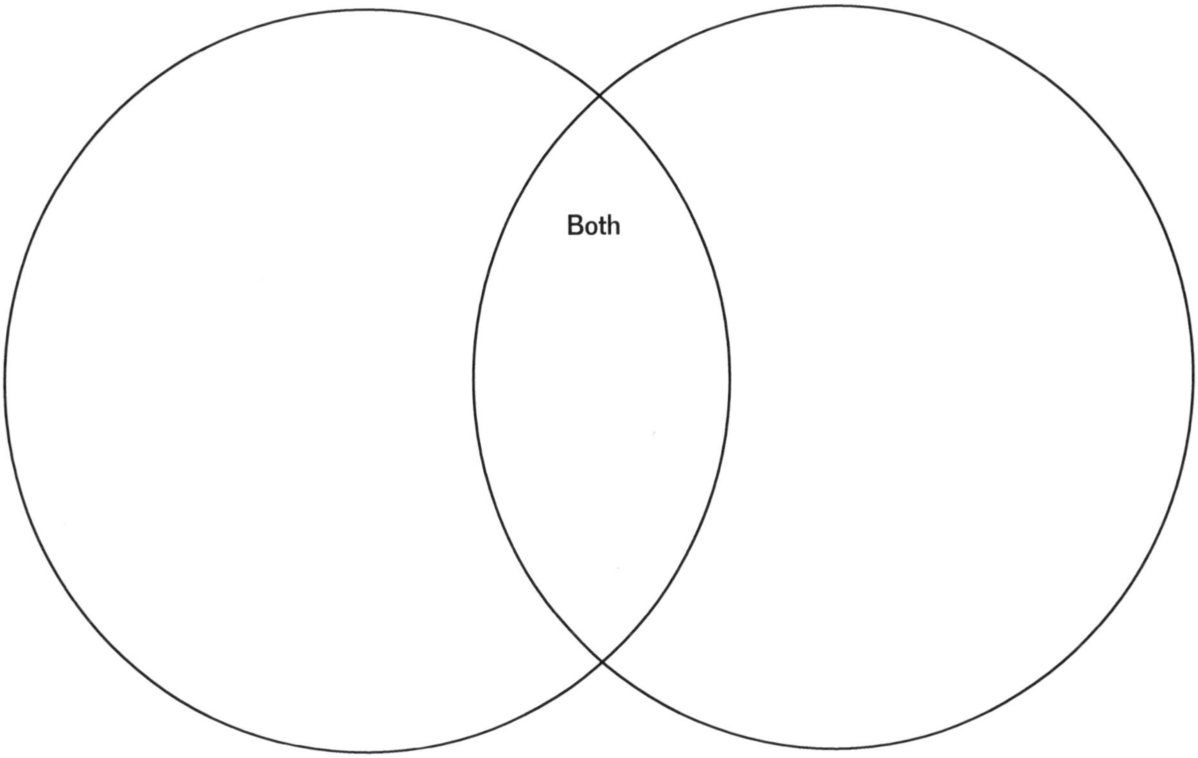

Name ______________________ Date ______________ REPRODUCIBLE **BLM 9**

Chapter 5 Part 1: Fact and Opinion Chart

DIRECTIONS: Study the reading on pages 108–110. Fill in the "Fact" column with specific, true ideas from the reading passage. Put your opinions about each fact in the "Opinion" column.

TITLE: ______________________________

FACT	OPINION

Name ______________________ Date ______________ REPRODUCIBLE BLM 10

Chapter 5 Part 1: Automobile Survey

DIRECTIONS: Fill in the survey by interviewing five students in your class. Take notes and create your own comparison chart based on the data you collect from your interviews.

Question	Student 1	Student 2	Student 3	Student 4	Student 5
Do you have a car? If not, what method of transportation do you use?					
What kind of car do you have or want?					
How is it powered? *Example:* gas, electricity, hybrid					
Why did you choose your car? *Example:* cost, color, price, model, low maintenance, fuel efficiency?					
Do you like your car? Why? Why not?					

Chapter 5 Part 3: *Blog* Research Chart

DIRECTIONS: Find a *blog* (*weblog*) on a topic that interests you. You can find listings of *blogs* by using a search engine and typing in the words *blogs*, *blog* listings, or *blog research*. Answer as many questions as you can in the chart below. Be prepared to present your findings to the class.

What is the name of the *blog*?	
Who created it? Why?	
What did you infer about the person who created the *blog*?	
What is the topic of the *blog*?	
What were some interesting facts you learned about the topic?	
Did the *blog* include any specialized terms related to the topic?	
Did the *blog* include links to any other sites or *blogs*? If so, what were they about?	
What is your opinion of this *blog*?	

Chapter 6 Part 1: Noun Suffix Clusters

DIRECTIONS: Fill in each cluster diagram by putting a noun suffix in the middle and examples of nouns using the suffix in the smaller circles. Some noun suffixes to choose from: ***-ist*, *-er/-or*, *-ance/-ence*, *-ness*, *-sion/-tion*, *-ment*, *-ity***

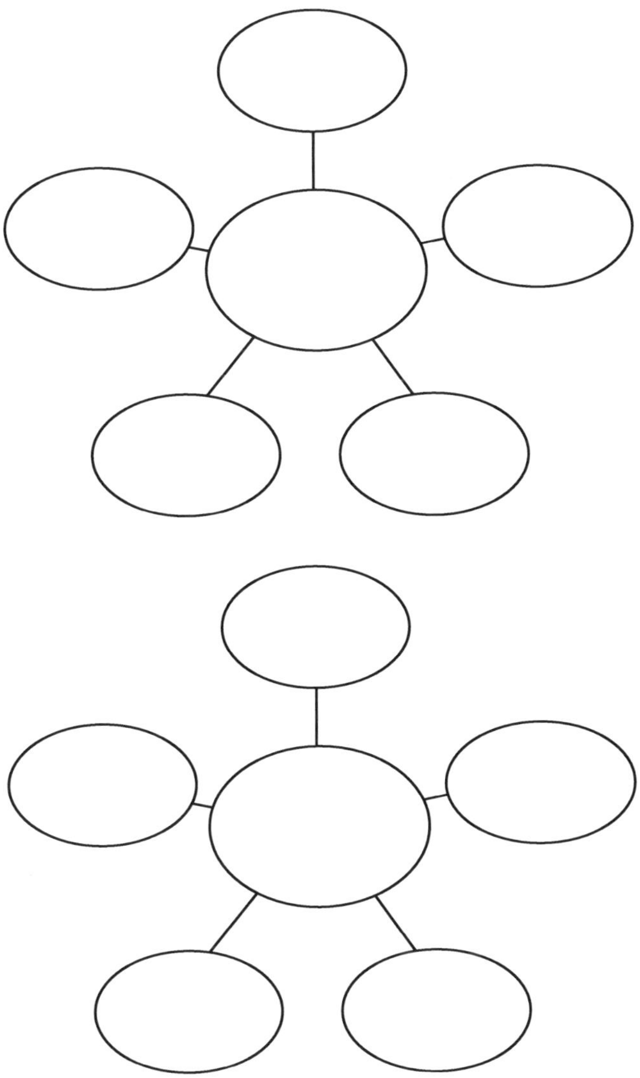

Name ______________________ Date ______________ REPRODUCIBLE BLM 13

Chapter 6 Part 1: Pizzeria Marketing Plan Outline

DIRECTIONS: Use the outline below to help you create a marketing plan for a pizzeria. Prepare to present your group's plan to the class.

1. **Our Pizza Company's Name:** ______________________
2. **Our Market:**
   - Who are we marketing to (type of people, i.e. students, housewives, etc.)
     ____
   - Do we have an eat-in restaurant or delivery?
     ____
   - Where are we located?
     ____
3. **Our Competition:**
   - Who is our main competition?
     ____
   - How will we be different from our competition?
     ____
4. **Our Pizza:**
   - What is special about our pizza?
     ____
   - Do we sell any other products?
     ____
5. **Our strengths and weaknesses:** ______________________
   ____
6. **Our Goals and Strategies:**
   - How will we tap a new market?
     ____
   - What is our pricing strategy? Do we offer specials such as "Buy 2, Get 1 Free?" What other specials do we offer?
     ____
   - How many outlets will we have?
     ____
   - Will we be a chain?
     ____
7. **Our Action Plan:**
   - Where will we advertise and how?
     ____
     ____

Chapter 6 Part 2: Futures

In one year, I will be...

In 5 years, I will be...

In 10 years, I will be...

Name ______________________ Date ______________ REPRODUCIBLE BLM 15

Chapter 7 Part 1: Confucius Says, We Say!

DIRECTIONS: Work with a group. Look at the statements in the "Confucius Says!" column and decide what they mean. Then write some statements in the "We Say!" column based on your group's philosophies.

Confucius Says!	We Say!
Actions committed by a person build society.	
Attempts to obtain short-term pleasure are bad while long-term goals make life better.	
Do the proper thing at the proper time.	
Do the right thing for the right reason.	
Mourn your father and mother for three years after their death.	
Treat your inferiors as you would want your superiors to treat you.	

Name ____________________ Date ____________ REPRODUCIBLE BLM 16

Chapter 7 Part 1: Word Family Charts

DIRECTIONS: Complete the charts with the proper parts of speech. You can choose from the list below or choose your own words.

ROOT WORDS: commit, resign, endure, perceive, innovate, express, beauty, friend, select

Root Word	Noun	Adjective	Verb
select	selection	selective	select
commit	commitment		commit
friend			

Root Word	Noun	Adjective	Verb

Root Word	Noun	Adjective	Verb

Chapter 8 Part 1: KWL Chart

DIRECTIONS: Before you begin reading, fill in the first two columns. Fill in the last column after you complete the reading.

Remember KWL stands for:

K: What I KNOW

W: What I WANT to know

L: What I LEARNED

Reading Passage: *Pure Genius*

K	W	L

Name ______________________ Date ______________ REPRODUCIBLE **BLM 18**

Chapter 9 Part 1: Venn Diagram: Cultural Comparisons

DIRECTIONS: Write the cultural topic you chose on the line below. Then write the names of the two cultures you chose on the lines above the Venn diagram. Then, fill in the diagram with the differences and similarities you discovered through your research. When you have finished, discuss the two questions with a partner.

Topic: ______________________________

Culture 1: ____________________ **Culture 2:** ____________________

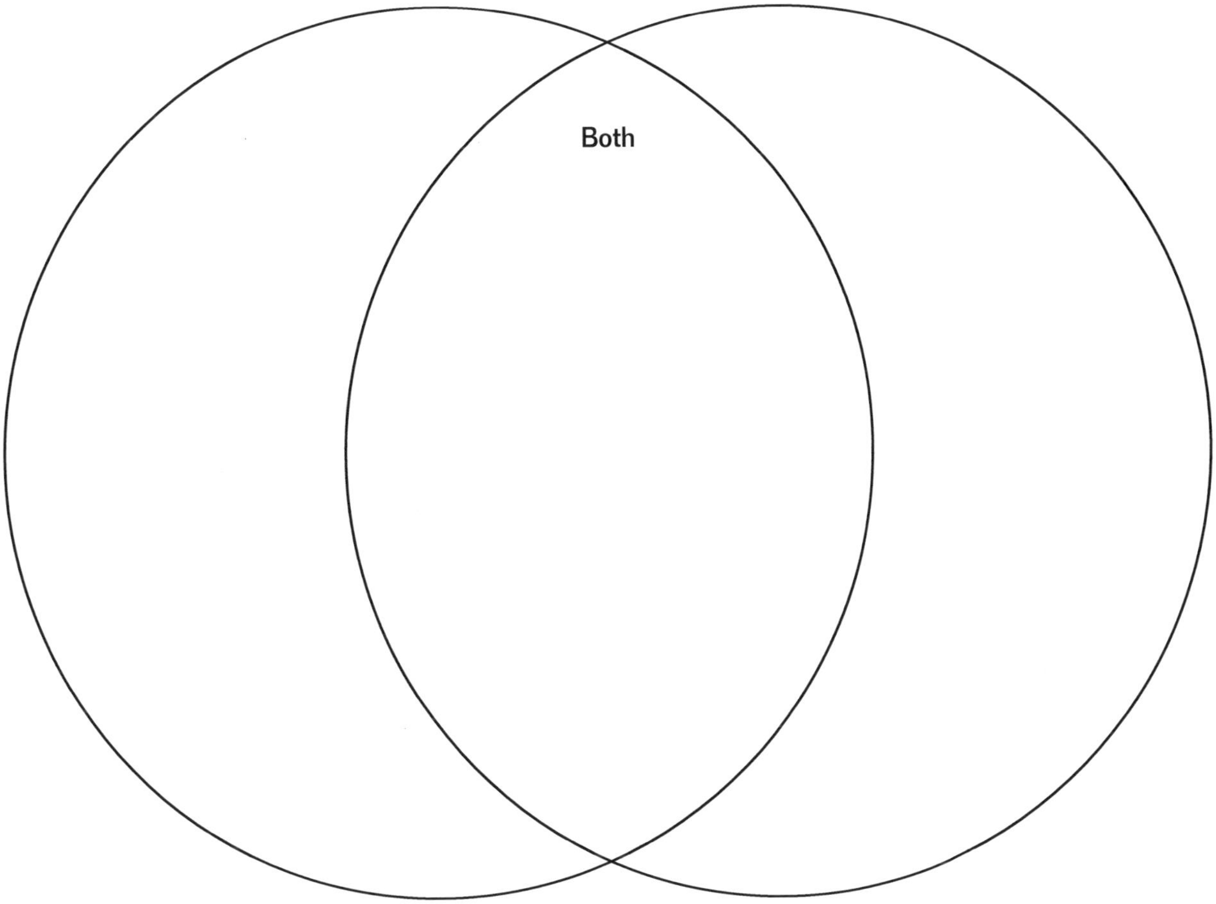

1. What things do the two cultures have in common with regards to your topic?
2. What are some ways the two cultures are different with regards to your topic?

Chapter 9 Part 2: Story Map

DIRECTIONS: Complete the story map with information from "A Clean Well-Lighted Place". Then compare your story map with your partner's.

TITLE:

AUTHOR:

SETTING/BRIEF DESCRIPTION:

CHARACTER/BRIEF DESCRIPTION:

CHARACTER/BRIEF DESCRIPTION:

EVENT: → EVENT: → EVENT: → EVENT:

PROBLEM:

RESOLUTION:

CONCLUSION:

GENERAL THEME:

Name ______________________ Date ______________ REPRODUCIBLE BLM 20

Chapter 10 Part 1: Ranking Crimes

DIRECTIONS:

Step 1: Think of ten crimes and list them on the Crime List below.

Step 2: Decide which crime is the most serious and mark the corresponding letter (A, B, C, etc.) closest to "most serious" on the continuum. Rank all the letters in order from most serious to least serious.

Step 3: Copy the crimes in order from most serious to least serious into the "CRIME" column of the Crime Rank chart.

Step 4: Finally, write what you think is an appropriate punishment for each crime in the "PUNISHMENT" column.

Crime List

A. ______________________ F. ______________________

B. ______________________ G. ______________________

C. ______________________ H. ______________________

D. ______________________ I. ______________________

E. ______________________ J. ______________________

Continuum Scale

Most serious |—|—|—|—|—|—|—|—|—| Least serious

Crime Rank

CRIME	PUNISHMENT
1. (Most serious)	
2.	
3.	
4.	
5.	
6.	
7.	
8.	
9.	
10. (Least serious)	

Name ______________________ Date ______________ REPRODUCIBLE **BLM 21**

Chapter 10 Part 2: Story Elements Chart

DIRECTIONS: Fill in the organizer with at least three details from the story, "Eye Witnesss" for each section.

TITLE ______________________________

Setting	
Main Characters	
Plot/Problems	
Solution	
Theme	

Name ______________________ Date ______________ REPRODUCIBLE BLM 22

Chapter 10 Part 2: Story Sequence Map ("Eye Witness")

DIRECTIONS: Fill in the story sequence map with key elements of the story's plot.

Setting:
↓
Conflict:
↓
Complications:
↓
Climax:
↓
Ending:

BLM #1 Answer Key

1. **C:** bedroom **2. I:** blackberry **3. A:** friendship
4. **J:** sweetheart **5. H:** basketball **6. F:** mailbox
7. **G:** wildlife **8. E:** wristwatch **9. B:** armchair
10. **D:** sunlight

New Words: Answers will vary.

BLM #3 Answer Key

Idiom Puzzles

Idioms from the David Beckham autobiography

took	a	knock	or	two		
In	a	comfort	zone			
whisked	off					
didn't	really	have	a	clue		
bracing	myself					
twist	in	the	pit	of	my	stomach
get	the	drift				
be	our	night				
feel	at	home				

Idioms related to baseball

get	to	first	base	
be	off	base		
strike	out			
play	ball			
throw	a	curve	ball	
play	hard	ball		
make	a	ballpark	estimate	
hit	the	home	stretch	
two	strikes	against	him	
step	up	to	the	plate

BLM #6 Answer Key

1. obsession
2. dissatisfaction
3. conventional *or* unconventional
4. grooming
5. attraction
6. possession(s)
7. appearance
8. unchanging
9. dissimilar
10. dependent
11. corresponding *or* correspondent
12. researcher
13. disproportionate
14. drawing
15. pleasantness *or* unpleasant

BLM #12 Answer Key

Possible answers: Cluster for **-tion/-sion** (in center circle): *globalization, emission, transmission, compensation, innovation.* Cluster for **-ment**: *management, requirement, environment, movement, settlement.* Cluster for **-ity**: *brevity, formality, humidity, nationality, prosperity.*

BLM #16 Answer Key

Word Family Chart

Possible answers:

Root Word	Noun	Adjective	Verb
select	selection	selective	select
commit	commitment	committed	commit
friend	friendship	friendly	befriend

Root Word	Noun	Adjective	Verb
beauty	beauty	beautiful	beautify
resign	resignation	resigned	resign
endure	endurance	endurable, enduring	endure

Root Word	Noun	Adjective	Verb
perceive	perception	perceptive	perceive
innovate	innovation	innovative	innovate
express	expression	expressive	express

BLM #19 Answer Key

Story Map

TITLE: "A Clean, Well-Lighted Place"

AUTHOR: Ernest Hemingway

SETTING/BRIEF DESCRIPTION: café, late at night, dark, shadowy

CHARACTER/BRIEF DESCRIPTION: old man—lonely, sitting alone, deaf, drinking, sometimes doesn't pay his bill

CHARACTER/BRIEF DESCRIPTION: waiter #1—young, talks a lot, married, unsympathetic

EVENT: → EVENT: → EVENT: → EVENT:

Possible answers:

PROBLEM: The young waiter does not sympathize with the old man and is in a hurry to go home. The old waiter sympathizes with the old man and is willing to let him stay as long as he wants in the café.

RESOLUTION: The old waiter explains his point of view to the young waiter.

CONCLUSION: All three characters leave the café.

GENERAL THEME: Some people have understanding and compassion for others and some don't.

BLM #21 Answer Key

Story Elements Charts ("Eye Witness")

Answers will vary. Possible answers:

Title: "Eye Witness"

Setting: the scene of the crime, the police station

Main characters: Struthers (the witness), Magruder, the narrator (Detective Cappeli), Lieutenant Anderson, Lieutenant Anderson's wife (the victim)

Plot/problems: Lieutenant Anderson's wife is mugged and murdered. The victim, Struthers, is afraid to talk about what he saw.

Solution: Struthers runs out of the police station when he sees Lieutenant Anderson. The reader must decide what happened.

Theme: This story is a murder mystery.

BLM #22 Answer Key

Story Sequence Map ("Eye Witness")

Answers may vary. Possible answers:

Setting: the police station

Conflict: Struthers is hesitant to talk about what he saw.

Complications: Struthers only wants to speak to lieutenant. He is afraid. The victim was married to the lieutenant.

Climax: Struthers agrees to help identify the murderer. The lieutenant enters the room and they look at each other.

Ending: Struthers runs out of the police station.

Name ______________________ Date ______________ Score ______________

CHAPTER 1 Test Mosaic 1 Reading

The Challenges of Multiple Births

SECTION I Reading Comprehension Read the passage. Then answer the questions that follow. *(5 points each)*

A Although multiple births are still relatively rare, in vitro fertilization has brought about a sharp increase in the number of "multiples"—twins, triplets, and quadruplets. In the past, couples who were not able to have children could either remain childless or adopt a child. However, some were reluctant to adopt because they were not comfortable with the idea of taking in a "stranger's" child. Others had a very strong desire for their own biological offspring. With the development of in vitro fertilization, many of these couples are now able to have biological children of their own. Between 1980 and 2000, the number of twins born in the United States increased by 74%. At the same time, the number of higher order multiples—triplets or more—increased by 500%.

B Multiple births can be very challenging for the mother-to-be. Imagine having several infants developing in a space designed for one. Although some of these women experience no problems, many have difficult pregnancies. Some mothers find themselves feeling extremely tired and short of breath. This is because the developing babies require a lot of iron and the mother begins to experience an iron deficiency. In order to carry the additional weight, her feet may grow as much as one shoe size. The shape of her body may also change permanently. As the babies develop, they push out the rib cage, expanding the size of her abdomen. To carry the additional weight, the thighs often become heavier. Despite a prescribed exercise program, these changes in body shape often remain after the pregnancy.

C And it's not just the mothers who are affected. Many multiple-birth children face physical and other types of challenges as well. Many are premature babies and will spend months in the hospital before they can go home. If the respiratory system is underdeveloped, the baby may have trouble breathing. If the nervous system is not fully developed, the child may be born with cerebral palsy. Later in life, learning difficulties sometimes emerge. The good news is that medical science is constantly uncovering ways to help these tiny infants survive and thrive.

D After the initial shock of having several children at once wears off, the parents-to-be are soon struck by the financial realities. "Oh, no! We can't afford five children!" they cry. However, most of these families make out just fine. People donate clothing, diapers, cribs, and baby food. Community groups raise money so the family can add living space to their house. Grocery stores come up with special discounts. Over time, these families somehow manage to survive. And with all the extra love in the house, money becomes less and less of an issue as time goes on.

1. What is the main idea of paragraph B?
   - (A) Changes in body shape often remain after the pregnancy.
   - (B) A woman's shoe size may increase during pregnancy.
   - (C) Multiple births can cause problems for the mother.
   - (D) Mothers of multiples should follow an exercise program after the pregnancy.
2. The number of twins born in the U.S. increased by what percentage between 1980 and 2000?
   - (A) 200%
   - (B) 500%
   - (C) 20%
   - (D) 74%
3. In paragraph C, the word *premature* probably means ______.
   - (A) slow
   - (B) early
   - (C) healthy
   - (D) difficult
4. In paragraph C, the word *emerge* probably means ______.
   - (A) appear
   - (B) get worse
   - (C) survive
   - (D) disappear
5. In paragraph D, which of the following is an example of an emotional reaction?
   - (A) Money becomes less of an issue.
   - (B) Community groups raise money for the family.
   - (C) We can't afford five children!
   - (D) Families somehow manage to survive.

SECTION II Strategy Choose the correct answer. *(5 points each)*

1. The main idea of paragraph A is not stated, it is implied. What is the implied main idea of paragraph A?
   - (A) Childless couples used to have two choices.
   - (B) The increase in multiple births is a result of in vitro fertilization.
   - (C) Most couples want children.
   - (D) Multiple births are becoming more common.
2. In paragraph B, which of the following is an example following up on the main idea?
   - (A) Multiple births are challenging for the mother.
   - (B) The mother's iron level often falls.
   - (C) Some women experience no problems.
   - (D) Several infants can develop in the space designed for one.

3. Which of the following statements can be inferred from the information in paragraph B?
   (A) Multiple births are easy for most mothers-to-be.
   (B) Developing babies don't require a lot of iron.
   (C) Multiple birth babies often have large rib cages
   (D) Women who have multiple births often can't wear the same clothes they wore before the births.

4. In paragraph D, the word *donate* probably means ______.
   (A) buy
   (B) give
   (C) sell
   (D) lend

5. What is the implied main idea of paragraph D?
   (A) The financial problems are hard to overcome.
   (B) People donate things to help these families.
   (C) Stores often help these families.
   (D) Money is not usually a terrible problem for these families.

SECTION III New Words Use the words in the box to complete the sentences below. *(3 points each)*

channel	estimated	founder	reveal	sustain
countryside	finite	infrastructure	slums	traditional

1. I prefer ______________ architecture. I think that modern buildings are not very interesting.
2. The ______________ is not deep enough for large boats.
3. In this city, there are a few ______________ full of poor and hungry people.
4. There is a(n) ______________ amount of water on Earth; there will never be anymore.
5. Steve Jobs was the ______________ of Apple Inc.
6. The engineers are not sure of the cost to build the highway, but they said it is a(n) ______________ $2 billion.
7. The archaeologists are conducting an expedition and a dig. They expect to ______________ an ancient city.
8. Tom wants to move to the ______________ to get away from the noise of the traffic.
9. Without better highways and other ______________, the country will not be able to modernize and advance.
10. Without additional money, the town cannot ______________ its economic growth.

SECTION IV Building Vocabulary Write the two words that make up each compound word. *(2 points each)*

1. handshake ____________ ____________
2. overcrowded ____________ ____________
3. countryside ____________ ____________
4. wildlife ____________ ____________
5. springtime ____________ ____________
6. snowfield ____________ ____________
7. humpback ____________ ____________
8. bighorn ____________ ____________
9. teahouse ____________ ____________
10. waterway ____________ ____________

TOTAL ____/100 pts.

Name ______________________ Date ______________ Score ______________

CHAPTER 2 Test Mosaic 1 Reading

A Look at Teamwork and Competition

SECTION I Reading Comprehension Read the passage. Then answer the questions that follow. *(5 points each)*

A Finding a balance between teamwork and competition is the key to success in a wide variety of fields. Medical research is one such area. Its discoveries have serious and wide-ranging effects. To do their best work, scientists are learning how to motivate themselves through competition with their colleagues, while at the same time doing a healthy amount of sharing information. The same principle holds true in business settings and in university classrooms. And research has recently uncovered another situation in which this balance is very important. It is a key element in helping twins develop as successful and independent individuals.

B People who study the nature of business organizations have come up with the term "M-Form." It refers to the type of organization that is carefully constructed to maintain a balance between teamwork and competition. M-Form companies are made up of many different divisions that compete against each other for money and other resources. However, these same competing divisions must also work as a team—sharing laboratories, marketing staff, and production facilities. M-Form companies are not directed from the top down. Each division sets its own direction and makes its own decisions. Management's role is to put together an overall plan that is in the best interests of the whole company.

C In terms of teamwork and competition, scientific researchers sometimes find themselves between a rock and a hard place (in a difficult situation without a simple solution). For example, scientists at several different universities and commercial laboratories may be researching ways to cure a particular type of cancer. They all describe some of what they are doing at conferences and in journals. This sharing helps all of them make advances in their research. In some ways, this puts them on the same team. On the other hand, there is sometimes fierce competition among colleagues to get credit for a discovery in order to increase their own prestige. In addition, commercial laboratories may have a lot of money tied up in their research. They may not want to share what they've spent millions of dollars to discover. In these cases, the agencies involved must do a lot of careful thinking about the proper balance between teamwork and competition.

D Another fascinating example of ongoing teamwork and competition involves the lives of identical twins. Most twins are constantly compared to each other on everything from school grades to athletic ability. This competition has a special edge to it. It is not only about winning, but also about creating a separate identity. Most twins are able to work out what seems to be a highly productive balance. For Jake Adams, a member of his college tennis team, beating his twin, Jerry, is really important. However, if the two are playing doubles, they are a tough team to beat!

1. What is the main idea of paragraph A?
   - (A) Teamwork and competition improve classroom learning.
   - (B) Teamwork and competition among scientists yields good results.
   - (C) Teamwork and competition are important in a variety of situations.
   - (D) Businesses can use teamwork and competition to become more successful.
2. The word *principle* in paragraph A means ______.
   - (A) most important
   - (B) rule
   - (C) problem
   - (D) leader
3. What is the main idea of paragraph C?
   - (A) Universities and laboratories often compete with each other.
   - (B) Researchers can learn a lot from each other's discoveries.
   - (C) Researchers sometimes have a hard time balancing teamwork and competition.
   - (D) Commercial laboratories sometimes don't want to share their discoveries.
4. According to the reading, which resource do divisions in M-From companies NOT have to share?
   - (A) laboratories
   - (B) workspace
   - (C) marketing staff
   - (D) production facilities
5. The phrase *work out* in paragraph D means ______.
   - (A) solve
   - (B) do exercises
   - (C) disagree about
   - (D) create

SECTION II Strategy Choose the correct answer. *(5 points each)*

1. Which of the following does scanning NOT involve?
   - (A) reading word for word
   - (B) thinking of what you are looking for
   - (C) moving your eyes quickly through the text
   - (D) stopping to write down information
2. Which of the following sentences contains a metaphor?
   - (A) The company was made up of several divisions.
   - (B) They made advances in their research.
   - (C) They found themselves between a rock and a hard place.
   - (D) There is fierce competition among colleagues.

3. Which compound adjective CANNOT modify the noun *book*?

(A) low-price
(B) best-selling
(C) good-tasting
(D) well-known

4. In paragraph C, *fierce* probably means ______.

(A) mean
(B) easy
(C) strange
(D) difficult

5. In paragraph D, *beat* probably means ______.

(A) get
(B) reduce
(C) defeat
(D) research

SECTION III New Words Fill in the blanks with words from the box. *(3 points each)*

ascend	job	low-end	revenues	V.P.
global	leading-edge	nondescript	get the drift	vicious

1. The reporter was ______________. She would not stop asking questions even though the interviewee was upset.
2. Many businessmen wear ______________ suits to work. They never wear new styles or bright colors.
3. I know it doesn't pay a lot, but I really need this ______________.
4. The company raised their prices in order to increase ______________.
5. My boss is a ______________. She hopes to become president someday.
6. I work for a ______________ corporation with offices in 16 different countries.
7. Several Japanese companies are ______________ producers of small cars.
8. I didn't buy a ______________ TV. My new flat-screen TV cost over $3000.
9. It will take us over three hours to ______________ this mountain.
10. Anne thought that by not returning John's calls that he would ______________ that she didn't want to see him anymore, but he still kept calling her.

SECTION IV Building Vocabulary Mark each sentence with a *T* for *true* or an *F* for *false*. *(2 points each)*

1. ______ *Earnings* is a synonym for *profit*.

2. ______ *Cut* is a synonym for *slice*.

3. ______ *Fail* is an antonym for *rally*.

4. ______ *Interrupt* is a synonym for *cut in*.

5. ______ *Office* is a synonym for *factory*.

6. ______ *Cry* is a synonym for *chant*.

7. ______ *Expensive* is an antonym for *low-cost*.

8. ______ *Feel comfortable* is a synonym for *feel at home*.

9. ______ *Don't like* is a synonym for *don't have a clue*.

10. ______ *Dance around* is an antonym for *cavort*.

TOTAL ______ /100 pts.

Name ______________________ Date ______________ Score ______________

CHAPTER 3 Test Mosaic 1 Reading

Building Strong Relationships

SECTION I Reading Comprehension Read the passage. Then answer the questions that follow. *(5 points each)*

A Like everything else in modern life, relationships have become the focus for extensive scientific study. This has resulted in the development of a plethora of organizations, self-surveys, magazine articles, books, and websites designed to help people learn how to have healthier, more enjoyable relationships.

B The Washington, DC-based organization, Advocates for Youth, puts out information on how families can build stronger relationships among their members. After extensive study, this group came up with a list of the features that make for a happy, nurturing family life. The first trait on the list is commitment. When people put family first—before work or school activities or outside friendships—strong family relationships result. The second mark of a close family is appreciation. Family members who express affection for each other, and look for the positive not the negative, become much closer over time. A third important characteristic is simply time spent together as a family. Some busy parents make sure to spend small amounts of "quality time" with their children each week, but the research shows that the *quantity* of time also really matters a great deal. It takes time to develop and maintain strong, loving relationships. They don't grow out of spending half an hour together twice a week.

C Psychologists who study marriage have found that one way to help guarantee a happy marriage is to use a prenuptial survey. One instrument that has received a lot of attention is the Premarital Personal Relationship Survey, nicknamed "Prepare." This questionnaire was created by University of Minnesota family psychology professor, David Olson. Originally it consisted of a few simple questions. The couple would then share their individual results with each other and discuss their similarities and differences. The test has since expanded to include 165 carefully-designed queries which clarify each person's attitudes toward money, sex, leisure time, children, and many other crucial areas. In some places, clergy won't marry a couple unless they complete the survey process together. Their aim is to create happier marital relationships and to help avoid marriages in which the couple has little chance for happiness together.

D A website sponsored by the Contra Costa County school system in California provides guidance to teachers who want to help their students develop better interpersonal relationship with peers, school staff, and family members. The site shows teachers how to incorporate social skills training into language arts instruction. It demonstrates how to use stories, poems, and writing assignments in regular English textbooks to focus on such skills as showing respect, resolving conflict, and giving compliments. This focus on building relationships doesn't take time away from academic instruction, and it increases the chances for the students' personal success and happiness.

1. In paragraph A, the word *plethora* probably means ______.
   (A) group
   (B) few
   (C) wide variety
   (D) club
2. In paragraph B, how many traits of strong families are discussed?
   (A) one
   (B) two
   (C) three
   (D) four
3. What is the main idea of paragraph C?
   (A) Prenuptial surveys help guarantee a happy marriage.
   (B) Prenuptial surveys must be long to work well.
   (C) Many clergy require that couples take a prenuptial survey before getting married.
   (D) Couples who don't take a prenuptial survey have little chance for happiness.
4. What is the main idea of paragraph D?
   (A) The website makes use of textbooks.
   (B) Students do reading and writing assignments.
   (C) Students learn to show respect and give compliments.
   (D) The website helps teachers know how to help students learn social skills.
5. In paragraph D, the word *interpersonal* probably means ______.
   (A) between two people
   (B) impersonal
   (C) large-group
   (D) secret

SECTION II Strategy Choose the correct answer. *(5 points each)*

1. Which of the following does reading a chart for information NOT involve?
   - (A) Move your eyes quickly until you find the information you want.
   - (B) Write down all the important ideas you find.
   - (C) Ignore information that doesn't answer the question you're working on.
   - (D) Skim for the general idea.
2. Choose the most general statement below.
   - (A) Many websites help families learn how to build stronger relationships.
   - (B) Many websites contain surveys that help couples analyze their relationships.
   - (C) Many websites feature information about building relationships.
   - (D) Many websites describe ways that teachers can help students relate better.
3. Which of the following does skimming NOT involve?
   - (A) summarizing the idea in a single sentence
   - (B) looking at headings
   - (C) looking at photos
   - (D) noting the title
4. Choose the most specific statement below.
   - (A) There are four men and twelve women in my "family living" class.
   - (B) There are sixteen people in my "family living" class.
   - (C) Most of the students in my "family living" class are women.
   - (D) All of the students in my "family living" class have at least two children.
5. What does writing down the key points in a summary NEVER involve?
   - (A) the author's opinion
   - (B) main ideas
   - (C) important facts
   - (D) your opinion

SECTION III New Words Match each word with its definition. Write the letter of the definition in the blank. *(4 points each)*

Words		Definitions
1. _______ entreat	a.	twisted and turned
2. _______ summon	b.	to accept
3. _______ writhed	c.	to trick (someone) just for fun
4. _______ legible	d.	readable
5. _______ frantic	e.	to beg (someone) to say yes
6. _______ speak your mind	f.	someone who doubts something
7. _______ skeptic	g.	to call
8. _______ play a farce	h.	belongings
9. _______ abide	i.	to express your real thoughts
10. _______ possessions	j.	overly excited

SECTION IV Building Vocabulary Read the groups of word. Two words in each group are from the same family. Cross out the word that does NOT belong. *(2 points each)*

1. attractive	attraction	attribute
2. dependent	deepen	independence
3. passing	passion	passionate
4. appearance	apparent	appearing
5. dissatisfaction	satisfy	faction

TOTAL ____/100 pts.

Name ______________________ Date ______________ Score ______________

CHAPTER 4 Test Mosaic 1 Reading

International Drug Research

SECTION I Reading Comprehension Read the passage. Then answer the questions that follow. *(5 points each)*

A The 2005 film *The Constant Gardener*, directed by Fernando Meirelles and based upon John le Carré's novel, brought popular attention to another problematic aspect of globalization: international drug research. The film tells the story of Justin Quayle, a low-level British diplomat stationed in Kenya, whose wife is suddenly killed. As he looks for her murderers, he discovers the dangerous research a European drug company is conducting on poor Africans. His wife had discovered the same research. In order to create a safe tuberculosis drug to be sold in the West, a Dutch drug manufacturer has forced a community of villagers to participate in their tests. The villagers have been told that they would not receive any medical attention if they refuse. With the help of British and Kenyan officials on their payroll, the company covered up the many deaths caused by the research. When Justin's wife threatened to reveal them, they killed her.

B Although this is just a film, it presents some parallels with the real world. Western drug researchers, whether corporate or nonprofit, conduct tests on people in developing countries, such as Kenya in exchange for money or health care. Wealthier nations protect their citizens by requiring evidence that new drugs work safely and effectively before they allow them to be sold to the public. But the laws in these affluent countries make it difficult for drug companies to conduct tests on citizens. For example, the American drug company Pfizer went into Nigeria in 1996 when that country was suffering from a widespread epidemic of bacterial meningitis. At the time, Pfizer was trying to get approval from the US Food and Drug Administration (FDA) for its new antibiotic, Trovan. In the US, the company needed proof that Trovan, which was delivered in a pill form, would work as well as the standard antibiotic that was delivered through an injection needle. In order to receive this proof, Pfizer gave equal numbers of children the pill and the injection. At the end of the trial, both groups suffered the same number of deaths. Based on the high numbers of children in these test groups, the FDA gave the company approval to market oral Trovan to children with meningitis. Yet some critics claim that it was unethical to test an unproven drug in the middle of an epidemic. Others are disturbed by the fact that the injected drug was given in smaller quantities than usual.

C The ethical dilemma of this and similar cases is compounded by the fact that while new drugs are often tested in poor countries, their results are rarely applied or available there. Also, drug researchers seldom seek to prevent diseases like malaria, polio, and other common threats to good health in the developing world.

1. Western drug researchers work in the developing world in order to ______

(A) prevent diseases like malaria and polio.
(B) produce thrilling movies everybody will enjoy.
(C) save Nigerian children from dying of meningitis.
(D) prove that new drugs will safely and effectively cure sicknesses.

2. Critics of the American company Pfizer claim they received FDA approval for the new meningitis antibiotic Trovan by ______

(A) testing it against an inadequate dosage of the standard meningitis antibiotic.
(B) delivering it to patients in a pill form.
(C) delivering it to patients through an injection needle.
(D) making it difficult to conduct tests on their own citizens.

3. The word "corporate" in paragraph B probably means ______

(A) rich.
(B) poor.
(C) relating to business.
(D) not profitable.

4. Justin Quayle is ______

(A) a drug researcher.
(B) a current low-level Kenyan diplomat.
(C) a character in a movie.
(D) a tuberculosis patient.

5. The writer of the above passage ______

(A) is neutral toward the subject of international drug research.
(B) believes that international drug research will create a healthier world.
(C) is critical of international drug research.
(D) believes that all international drug research must stop now.

SECTION II Strategy Each question refers directly to certain words in the passage. Look back at them before you decide on your answers. *(5 points each)*

1. A different way to say that the film "brought popular attention to another problematic aspect of globalization" is: ______

(A) The film made people think critically about globalization.
(B) The film made globalization even more popular than it already is.
(C) The film has many different aspects.
(D) The film is very popular.

2. Another way to say the film has "some parallels with the real world" is: ______

(A) The film reflects something that is real.
(B) The film is not real at all.
(C) The film is made in the real world.
(D) The film is a documentary.

3. The word *affluent* is used in Paragraph B. What is a synonym for *affluent*?

(A) poor
(B) rich
(C) large
(D) small

4. Another way to say "The ethical dilemma of this and similar cases thickens" is: ______

(A) International drug research has proven to be more concerned with profits than with saving lives.
(B) International drug research continues to raise more and more questions on right and wrong.
(C) International drug research has proven to bring good health to the whole world.
(D) All of the above

5. Another way to say "Drug researchers seldom seek to prevent diseases like malaria, polio, and other common threats to good health in the developing world" is: ______

(A) Drug researchers are more concerned with diseases that are common in wealthy countries.
(B) Malaria and polio are easy to cure.
(C) Drug researchers are more concerned with diseases that are common in poor countries.
(D) People in wealthy countries suffer from malaria and polio.

SECTION III New Words Fill in the blanks with words from the box. *(3 points each)*

acquiring	affluent	benefits	communities	compensation
found	hence	physical	prevent	virtually

It is difficult to judge the ______ (1) of international drug research because there is so much controversy surrounding the issue.

There are many ______ (2) all over the world that do not have access to adequate health care.

What do you think would be fair ______ (3) for participating in a clinical test of a new drug?

______ (4) all nations stand to gain from more research into world health issues. Our sense of ______ (5) well-being is essential to leading productive lives.

The need to ______ (6) unethical research practices is very strong.

People in ______ (7) countries tend to take many things for granted. Since they have everything they want, they have ______ (8) little need to question where things come from.

______ (9) information about the business practices of large corporations is often very difficult and time-consuming, ______ (10) it is important to keep abreast of current events and the daily news.

SECTION IV Building Vocabulary Match the words on the left with the synonyms on the right. *(4 points each)*

1. ______ looks for
2. ______ goes on the trail
3. ______ manufacturer
4. ______ evidence
5. ______ epidemic

a. searches
b. contagious disease
c. proof
d. is assigned to
e. maker

TOTAL ______/100 pts.

Name ______________________ Date ______________ Score ______________

CHAPTER 5 Test Mosaic 1 Reading

Fiber Optic Technology

SECTION I Reading Comprehension Read the passage. Then answer the questions that follow. *(5 points each)*

A Fiber optic cables have many advantages over copper wire, which used to be the material of choice for transmitting telephone and other communication signals such as television from one point to another. To begin with, fiber optic cable is cheaper to manufacture than copper wire. Secondly, it is lighter and thinner, so it takes up less space. In addition, fiber optic cables distort the signals much less than copper wires do, and low-power transmitters can be used with fiber optics instead of the high-voltage transmitters needed for copper wires. That saves a lot of money. New fiber optic cables offer so many advantages that copper wire connections for telephones, television, the Internet, and other communication services may soon be a thing of the past.

B The main characteristics of fiber optic cables are that they are very flexible and deliver an extremely clear picture. This makes them invaluable in situations where very clear images are needed and space is severely limited. For this reason, many medical devices used inside the human body, including some that are used for surgery, feature fiber optic technology. Today, gall bladder operations can be performed using a laparoscope which contains a camera and tiny surgical tools connected to a viewing screen by fiber optic cables. There is no need for a large incision; the surgeon inserts the laparoscope containing a fiber optic cable through the belly button and takes out the gall bladder in tiny pieces.

C The part of the fiber optic cable that light travels though is called the *core*. It is the flexible glass center of the cable. Wrapped around the core is a layer called the *cladding*. It's purpose is to reflect all the light in the core back into the core without letting any escape. Wrapped around the cladding is yet another layer called the *buffer coating*. It protects the inside of each strand from damage and moisture. The cables you see running to your television set or connecting computers in an office are actually bundles of many separate fiber optic strands. What you see on the outside is called the *jacket*, the final covering that holds all the strands together.

D But just how does a fiber optic cable work? Imagine what it looks like to shine a flashlight down a long straight hall, lighting up the space. Then imagine that the hall suddenly has hundreds of twists and turns. How are you going to get that light to travel around corners? You can do it by lining the hall with mirrors. The cladding in a fiber optic cable is actually a mirrored surface that produces that same effect. *Optical generators* every half mile or so boost the power of the light signals. This combination delivers crystal clear images over distances of hundreds of miles.

1. What is the main idea of paragraph A?

Ⓐ Most communications signals used to be carried by copper wires.
Ⓑ Fiber optic cables are lighter and cheaper than copper wires.
Ⓒ Fiber optic cables have many advantages.
Ⓓ Copper wires may soon be a thing of the past.

2. What is the meaning of the word *invaluable* in paragraph B?

Ⓐ very useful
Ⓑ awkward
Ⓒ useless
Ⓓ expensive

3. The outer layer of a fiber optic cable is called the ______.

Ⓐ cladding
Ⓑ core
Ⓒ buffer coating
Ⓓ jacket

4. Which paragraph in the reading passage is organized from general to specific?

Ⓐ A
Ⓑ B
Ⓒ C
Ⓓ D

5. What is the meaning of *crystal clear* in paragraph D?

Ⓐ shiny
Ⓑ like a mirror
Ⓒ extremely accurate
Ⓓ moving

SECTION II Strategy Choose the correct answer. *(5 points each.)*

1. New fiber optic cables offer so many advantages that copper wire connections for telephones, television, the Internet, and other communication services may soon be a thing of the past. What does *a thing of the past* mean?

Ⓐ no longer used
Ⓑ a better way of doing things
Ⓒ an important part of the history of communications
Ⓓ very useful

2. The hurricane was so strong it blew the car over onto its roof. Which compound word means the same as *blew the car over onto its roof*?

Ⓐ overcame the car
Ⓑ upended the car
Ⓒ downloaded the car
Ⓓ undertook the car

3. What is the first step in creating an informal study outline?

Ⓐ Making a list of examples
Ⓑ Making a list of points with regular numbers
Ⓒ Writing a brief summary
Ⓓ Making a list of points with roman numerals

4. Which compound adjective best describes fiber optic cables?

Ⓐ low-tech
Ⓑ little-known
Ⓒ light-weight
Ⓓ high-priced

5. If you find a word you don't understand near the beginning of an article, what should you do?

Ⓐ Skim the whole article for general information and then return to the word.
Ⓑ Read the article two or three times and then return to the word.
Ⓒ Change the word to another part of speech.
Ⓓ Scan the article for a definition of the word.

SECTION III New Words Match each word with the correct definition. *(3 points each)*

1. _______ braking		a. form of transportation
2. _______ efficient		b. accept an electronic file
3. _______ data		c. add electricity to something
4. _______ scenario		d. plan
5. _______ charge		e. stopping
6. _______ handmade		f. side by side
7. _______ interwoven		g. well-organized
8. _______ download		h. closely connected
9. _______ vehicle		i. information
10. _______ parallel		j. not manufactured

SECTION IV Building Vocabulary Complete each sentence with the correct compound word from the box. *(2 points each)*

handmade	machine-washable	small-scale	timepiece	well-read
home-based	newlywed	speedway	top hat	worn out

1. Two hundred years ago, clothes were all ________________.
2. All of our furniture is very old and ________________.
3. Today most people buy only ________________ clothes because dry cleaning is expensive.
4. Professor Franklin knows a lot. She's a ________________ person.
5. It's a ________________ restaurant. There are only seats for ten people.
6. Linda just got married. She's a ________________.
7. My grandfather's watch is my favorite ________________.
8. My aunt makes birthday cakes in her house and sells them. She has a ________________ business.
9. At formal weddings the groom wears a tuxedo and a ________________.
10. My brother likes to race his car at a nearby ________________.

TOTAL ______ /100 pts.

Name ______________________ Date ______________ Score ______________

CHAPTER 6 Test Mosaic 1 Reading

The History of Money

SECTION I Reading Comprehension Read the passage. Then answer the questions that follow. *(5 points each)*

A The *Yen*, the *Dollar*, the *Quetzal*, or the *Peso*—no matter what the currency is called, money is an important part of life in nearly every culture today and has been throughout history. The concept of money dates back thousands of years. Originally, money did not consist of metal coins or paper bills. Rather, people paid for things with objects that were useful and therefore considered valuable. We sometimes call this *commodity money*. Some examples of commodity money used throughout history are iron nails, rare seashells, bread, and livestock, such as pigs or cattle.

B Salt and other spices were also once used as money. In fact, the word *salary* (the money that employees are paid weekly or monthly by their employers) is derived from the Latin word *salarium* meaning a payment made in salt. The expression *He's (not) worth his salt* is probably derived from this, because it was used to mean that someone's work was (or wasn't) worth the amount of money (or salt) he or she was being paid. There is also evidence that, during the Middle Ages, pepper was used as a form of money, hence the old French saying *As dear as pepper*. In England, one could actually pay one's rent in pepper! Even in more modern times commodity money has been used in cases where there was no access to actual currency. An example of this was during and after World War II in Europe, where tobacco was often used in place of money.

C Certain metals, such as gold, silver, and copper have been used as commodity money for thousands of years. Metals were exchanged in the form of jewelry and nuggets (small lumps) and eventually appeared in the form of coins around 560 B.C.E. The use of metals coins as money became widespread after the use of the touchstone was discovered. The touchstone enabled people to find how much of a certain type of metal was contained in a nugget and therefore determine its value. Eventually, the system of representative money emerged in the form of paper bills. This system is called *representative money*, because the paper itself is of very little intrinsic value, but is based on its correlation to a valued commodity, such as gold.

D Currencies and methods of transaction seem to be constantly evolving. An example of this is the use of *electronic money*, money that is transferred electronically. Thanks to modern technology and electronic money, people are now able to pay their bills, transfer funds from one account to another, and receive their paychecks from their employers without ever stepping into a bank. It looks like the concept of money is here to stay, but we are probably still in for more surprising changes in the future.

(source: http://en.wikipedia.org/wiki/History_of_money)

1. What is the main idea of the reading passage?

(A) Commodity money was used before coins and paper money.
(B) Money has always been an important part of life.
(C) Salt is a very valuable substance.
(D) Money will soon be a thing of the past.

2. According to the reading passage, when was pepper used as a form of commodity money in Europe?

(A) during World War II
(B) present day
(C) thousands of years ago
(D) during the Middle Ages

3. According to the reading passage, which item was often used in place of money in Europe after World War II?

(A) rare shells
(B) bread
(C) tobacco
(D) iron nails

4. In paragraph C, *determine* probably means ______.

(A) weigh
(B) decide
(C) increase
(D) test

5. Which of the following does the article NOT mention as something people can now do without going to a bank?

(A) pay their bills
(B) deposit their paychecks
(C) transfer funds
(D) buy food and clothing

SECTION II Strategies Choose the best answer. *(5 points each)*

1. In paragraph A, *considered* probably means ______.

(A) thought of
(B) traded
(C) valued
(D) represented

2. In paragraph B, the Latin word *salarium* means ______.

(A) salty
(B) valuable
(C) a payment in salt
(D) a touchstone

3. In paragraph B, *derived from* probably means ______.

(A) traded
(B) came from
(C) changed
(D) discovered

4. In paragraph B, *dear* probably means ______.

(A) small
(B) delicious
(C) valuable
(D) worthless

5. In paragraph C, *intrinsic* probably means ______.

(A) metallic
(B) expensive
(C) rare
(D) natural

SECTION III New Words Complete the sentences with the words below. *(4 points each)*

affordable	anticipated	enormous	mentality	succulent
amicable	convenience	inclined	specialities	transform

1. The new movie theater in downtown Los Angeles has 28 screens, making it the biggest movie theater in California. It's ____________________!
2. I was ____________________ to tell Marta that her outfit didn't match, but decided not to because she's very self-conscious as it is.
3. Many people consider shopping online to be a real ____________________, as it saves them from having to spend a lot of time in their cars and in shopping malls.
4. Karen has a very positive ____________________ and always sees the bright side of every situation. That's probably why she's always so happy.
5. The company's Chief Financial Officer increased our department's budget last year, because she ____________________ our sales would go up 10% over the previous year.
6. These strawberries are perfectly ripe. They are delicious and so ____________________!
7. James found that living in New York City was too expensive, so he decided to move somewhere where housing was more ____________________.
8. Even though Ana and Peter are divorced, their relationship is ____________________ and they still call each other on their birthdays.
9. It's amazing how new furniture can ____________________ a room. Our living room looks completely different!
10. That shop sells some delicious Italian ____________________, such as olives, fresh pasta, and many different kinds of cheese.

SECTION IV Building Vocabulary Match the word on the left with the suffix on the right that changes its part of speech. *(2 points each)*

1. danger ______	a. -ity
2. afford ______	b. -ion
3. protect ______	c. -able
4. power ______	d. -ous
5. technical ______	e. -ful

TOTAL ______/100 pts.

Name ______________________ Date ______________ Score ______________

CHAPTER 7 Test — Mosaic 1 Reading

The Life of Thurgood Marshall

SECTION I Reading Comprehension Read the passage. Then answer the questions that follow. *(4 points each)*

A Thurgood Marshall, born in Baltimore, Maryland in 1908, was the first African American to become a Justice of the United States Supreme Court. His grandfather had been a slave and he was raised by parents who were not yet themselves totally free of the limitations that race imposed upon blacks in American society. His father was a steward at an all-white country club and his mother taught in a segregated school. But his family saw his abilities and did everything possible to ensure his success in life.

B After graduating from Lincoln University in 1930, Marshall applied to the University of Maryland School of Law. At this time, however, the university still had a strict policy of racial segregation—only whites were allowed to attend. He next applied to Howard University, a well-respected, historically black university in Washington, D.C. Howard was not associated with any religious institution and was open to people of both sexes and of any race. He excelled in his studies there and after graduating in 1933 opened his own law practice in Baltimore. The next year he was involved in a lawsuit against the University of Maryland, the institution that had refused to allow him to attend their law school. He proved that the other universities that blacks were free to attend either did not have law schools or were in other ways unequal to the University of Maryland. Because of Marshall's hard work, the state courts ruled that the university must admit people of all races.

C Marshall continued to fight for racial equality all his life. As chief counsel for the National Association for the Advancement of Colored People (NAACP), he won many important cases that helped bring about the end of segregated educational systems in the U.S. On June 13, 1967, President Lyndon B. Johnson appointed Marshall to the Supreme Court. Although there were many objections, Johnson said that it was, "the right thing to do, the right time to do it, the right man and the right place." Marshall served on the court for twenty-four years compiling an impressive record that included strong support for constitutional protection of individual and civil rights.

D The good work that Marshall did during his life will not soon be forgotten. Several middle schools also bear his name, including those in St. Petersburgh, Florida and Marion, Indiana. His name was also given to the law schools at the University of Maryland and the University of California, San Diego. The Washington, D.C., airport is now called The Baltimore-Washington International Thurgood Marshall Airport. The Columbia Pike, a highway in Virginia, has been renamed the Thurgood Marshall Memorial Highway. And in 2006, the Episcopal Church even nominated him for sainthood.

1. In what year did the University of Maryland Law School begin admitting black students?

(A) 1930
(B) 1933
(C) 1934
(D) 1940

2. In paragraph B, the word *segregation* probably means _______.

(A) separation
(B) punishment
(C) equality
(D) awareness

3. Which quote from paragraph B disproves the following statement: *African Americans could attend any college they chose.*

(A) … Howard University, a well-respected, historically black university….
(B) … the university still had a strict policy of racial segregation.
(C) Howard… was open to people of both sexes and of any race.
(D) … the other universities that blacks were free to attend… did not have law schools . .

4. Which quote from paragraph C proves the following statement: *President Johnson totally supported the appointment of Marshall as a Supreme Court Justice.*

(A) … there were many objections…
(B) Marshall served on the court for twenty-four years…
(C) … President Lyndon B. Johnson appointed Marshall to the Supreme Court.
(D) … Johnson said that it was, "the right thing to do, the right time to do it, the right man and the right place."

5. What is the main idea of paragraph D?

(A) Marshall's memory has been honored in many different ways.
(B) Many schools have been named in Marshall's honor.
(C) Thurgood Marshall may become a saint.
(D) An airport and a highway have been named for Marshall.

STRATEGY II Strategy Read the sentences below. Choose the correct expressive word or phrase to replace the common words in italics. *(4 points each)*

1. Jonas Salk invented a vaccine that helped ______ (end) polio in children.
   (A) conclude
   (B) destroy
   (C) eradicate
   (D) finish off
2. Good food and enough sleep are ______ (sources) of good health.
   (A) realizations
   (B) promotions
   (C) backgrounds
   (D) cornerstones
3. The early death of a mother can ______ (upset) a young child.
   (A) be bothersome for
   (B) confuse
   (C) annoy
   (D) overwhelm
4. If you want to get good grades, you must be a ______ (serious) student.
   (A) nervous
   (B) diligent
   (C) perfect
   (D) knowledgeable
5. The Kennedys have become a famous political ______ (family).
   (A) dynasty
   (B) force
   (C) federation
   (D) component

SECTION III New Words Fill in the blanks with words from the box. *(3 points each)*

atone	compelling	influential	resigned	seized
commoners	founded	permeated	role	suppress

1. I spent a lot of time in my grandparent's home. They were very ______________ in my life.
2. Although I was very nervous, I tried to ______________ any outward signs of it.
3. After three years as president of the company, Mr. Harold ______________ last week.
4. It was a ______________ story. I finished the whole book in one sitting.
5. Mary George ______________ the first museum in our community.
6. The king never talked with the ______________.
7. The invading army ______________ the property of wealthy landowners.
8. The ______________ of a tutor is to help a student learn.
9. Danny wanted to ______________ for the harm he had caused his family.
10. The cigarette smoke ______________ the entire house.

SECTION IV Building Vocabulary Read the sentences below. In each blank, write a compound word, a word with a prefix, or a word with a suffix that means the same as the words in parentheses. *(3 points each)*

1. You can usually buy shampoo in a (store that sells drugs) ______________.
2. The house looks as if it is (not finished) ______________.
3. The book was so good I (read it a second time) ______________ it.
4. Most children enjoy playing (not indoors) ______________.
5. They usually play in the (yard that isn't the front yard) ______________.
6. Thurgood Marshall was a (person who defends) ______________ of the rights of all people.
7. At $50.00 each, these shirts are really (the opposite of underpriced) ______________!
8. Carla has to make an important (thing she has to decide) ______________ by Friday.
9. Where is the (clothes you wear when you're doing sports) ______________ department?
10. The local newspaper took a(n) (against the war) ______________ stand.

TOTAL ______ /100 pts.

Name ________________ Date ________________ Score ________________

CHAPTER 8 Test

Mosaic 1 Reading

Kala Ramnath

SECTION I Reading Comprehension Read the passage. Then answer the questions that follow. *(5 points each)*

A Although the modern-day violin was originally made in Italy in the 1700s, some say the first violin can be traced to an ancient Indian instrument called the Ravan Hatta. With such a rich musical history in India, it is not surprising that perhaps one of the most accomplished violin musicians in the world is India's remarkably talented Kala Ramnath. Born into a family of critically-acclaimed Indian musicians including violin legend Professor T.N. Krishnan, Kala demonstrated musical talent from childhood. She began playing when she was only three. At that time, she started her music education by studying under her grandfather, Vidwan Shri Narayan Lyer. Under his guidance, there was no room for laziness or excuses for not practicing, nor were there any breaks or trips outside of the home for leisure or fun. Kala's second teacher was her aunt, also a well-known violinist. Later, she moved on to study under high-profile musician Sangeet Martand Pandit Jasraj. With the help her three teachers, she mastered the techniques and the creative artistry that has set her apart from others.

B Although she learned the classical techniques with her teachers, Kala has since developed her own individual style. She uses unique bow and finger techniques to create notes that sound more like a human voice singing than a violin. These techniques have earned her violin the nickname of "The Singing Violin." She and her singing violin have toured the world extensively. Kala has performed in the United States, Greece, Australia, Canada, the United Arab Emirates, and Bangladesh.

C In addition to having toured in various parts of the world, she has also experimented with incorporating different types of sounds into her music. She has played with Ray Manzarek who played keyboards for the American rock band, The Doors, and with Eduardo Niebla, a Flamenco guitarist. She has also played alongside South Africa's Lucas Khumalo and Kúnlé Odutayo to create music with an African-Indian fusion.

D Kala has expanded her career beyond music into the areas of theater and radio broadcasting, where she has also excelled. She has gone beyond being thought of only as a musician to being a well-known personality in the worlds of TV and radio broadcasting. Although a pioneer in mixing her music with that of other cultures and genres, Kala is still, and always will be, considered an icon of North Indian classical music.

Source: http://www.kalaramnath.com/

1. The main idea of this article is that ______
   - (A) classical violin music is very popular in India.
   - (B) Kala's violin sounds like voices singing.
   - (C) Kala Ramnath is very talented.
   - (D) Kala is a famous radio and TV star.

2. The first modern-day violin was made in ______
   - (A) India.
   - (B) Italy.
   - (C) Bangladesh.
   - (D) South Africa.

3. How many violinists did Kala study under?
   - (A) 5
   - (B) 4
   - (C) 3
   - (D) 2

4. Why has Kala's violin been nicknamed "The Singing Violin"?
   - (A) She can make the violin sound like a voice singing.
   - (B) The violin sings.
   - (C) Kala sings while she plays.
   - (D) People sing to her music.

5. Kala has not worked with an artist from ______
   - (A) South Africa.
   - (B) Spain.
   - (C) United States.
   - (D) Bangladesh.

SECTION II Strategy This section refers directly to certain words in the passage. Look back at them before you decide on your answers. *(5 points each)*

1. In paragraph A, the word *remarkably* could be replaced with the word ______.
   - (A) curiously
   - (B) ordinarily
   - (C) noticeably
   - (D) interestingly
2. In paragraph A, what inference can be made about Kala?
   - (A) She enjoys traveling around the world.
   - (B) She works hard.
   - (C) She can play many musical instruments.
   - (D) She dislikes practicing the violin.
3. In paragraph B, what word could be used in place of *conventional*?
   - (A) unique
   - (B) traditional
   - (C) modern
   - (D) strict
4. Use the structure clues and context to guess the meaning of the word *fusion* in Paragraph D.
   - (A) a blend
   - (B) an ingredient
   - (C) a song
   - (D) a band
5. What inference can be made about Kala's grandfather?
   - (A) He was strict.
   - (B) He was lazy.
   - (C) He liked to play the violin.
   - (D) He didn't like music.

SECTION III New Words Use the words in the box to complete the sentences below. *(4 points each)*

architect	assumptions	contemporary	dud	mentor
articulate	be on the lookout	contraption	in retrospect	publish

1. Because he likes to design buildings, Kevin is studying to be a(n) ________________.
2. I am going to ________________ my first book; it's a biography of Thomas Edison.
3. Most of the buildings in the city are in a ________________ style; there are very few traditional ones.
4. If you are interested in reading a book about inventions, I will be ________________ when I go to the bookstore tomorrow.
5. What is that strange looking ________________? Is it a bike or a motorcycle or a boat?
6. You know… ________________, I probably should have studied biology in college instead of finance.
7. My first boss was a great ________________; she taught me all about design and how to succeed in business.
8. That invention was such a ________________; it didn't work at all.
9. It's hard for me to ________________ my thoughts out loud. Let me write them down instead. It will probably make things clearer.
10. You should be careful about making ________________. It's important to check to be sure something is true.

SECTION IV Building Vocabulary Match each adjective with its definition. Write the letter of the definition in the blank. *(2 points each)*

Adjectives	Definitions
1. _______ turbulent	a. new; modern
2. _______ isolated	b. theoretical; abstract
3. _______ contemporary	c. excited; stormy
4. _______ cavernous	d. set apart; alone
5. _______ conceptual	e. spacious; large and hollow

TOTAL ______/100 pts.

Name ______________________ Date ______________ Score ______________

CHAPTER 9 Test Mosaic 1 Reading

Culture Shock

SECTION I Reading Comprehension Read the passage. Then answer the questions that follow. *(5 points each)*

A Anyone who has spent time in another country has probably experienced some degree of *culture shock*. What is culture shock? The term was coined in 1958 to describe the feelings of anxiety, discomfort, and disorientation that people experience when moving to a new country and culture. Culture shock is said to have a few different stages, which set in after a person has spent a few weeks in the new environment. The first stage of culture shock is sometimes referred to as the "honeymoon" stage, because everything in the new culture is new and exciting. There are different foods to try, interesting places to visit and possibly a very different climate to experience. All of these things may seem exotic and thrilling for a little while, but this excitement eventually wears off.

B The second stage of culture shock occurs when the differences of the new environment start to seep in and are suddenly perceived as more irritating and disorienting than interesting and exciting. At this stage, many people tend to feel a sense of disconnectedness due to language problems and cultural miscommunications that they experience by doing everyday activities, such as taking public transportation and buying groceries. This stage is often characterized by the newcomer feeling angry and impatient and rejecting the new culture and its strange way of doing things.

C When people enter into the third stage of culture shock, they still experiences difficulties, but tend to deal with them with more patience and a sense of humor. Perhaps because they have had more of a chance to understand the culture they are in, they are more easily able to accept and appreciate its differences. At this stage, people also start to feel a sense of wanting to belong. In the fourth stage, people tend to truly feel a sense of belonging within the new culture and are able to accept the good and bad aspects of it. In addition to these four stages of culture shock, there is a fifth, which people may experience upon reentry to their native culture. This occurs when people discover that things changed while they were away. This is sometimes called *re-entry shock*.

D Although it is nearly impossible to avoid culture shock, there are things people can do in order to ease the stress they experience as a result of it. Here are a few suggestions that may help. Be patient. It's important to remember that adjusting to a new culture is a process that takes time. Maintain contact with the new culture by learning the language and getting involved in the community. Set some simple goals for yourself to help you see your progress. Remember that although living in a new culture can be very difficult, it can also be very rewarding!

Source: http://edweb.sdsu.edu/people/CGuanipa/cultshok.htm

1. What is the main idea of the reading passage?
   (A) Culture shock caused anxiety.
   (B) New places and cultures are very exciting at first.
   (C) Culture shock cannot be avoided.
   (D) There are different stages of culture shock.
2. The first stage of culture shock is sometimes referred to as the "honeymoon stage" because ______
   (A) people often spend their honeymoons in other countries.
   (B) everything is exciting and new.
   (C) there are lots of exotic flowers.
   (D) there are lots of everyday miscommunications.
3. According to the reading passage, people generally start feeling a sense of disconnectedness during the ______ stage of culture shock.
   (A) first
   (B) second
   (C) third
   (D) fourth
4. According to the reading passage, what do people often discover during the fifth stage of culture shock?
   (A) Things about their native culture changed while they were away.
   (B) They can no longer communicate in their native language.
   (C) They preferred the food in the "new" culture.
   (D) Their native culture seems boring and unfriendly.
5. Which of the items below does the reading passage NOT give as a suggestion for easing the stress of culture shock?
   (A) be patient
   (B) maintain contact with the new culture
   (C) set simple goals for yourself
   (D) avoid taking public transportation

SECTION II Strategies Use the context and your knowledge of word forms to choose the best meanings for the words in italics. *(5 points each)*

1. In paragraph A, the word *coined* probably means ______.
   (A) bought
   (B) changed
   (C) invented
   (D) described

2. In paragraph A, the word *thrilling* probably means ______.

(A) very exciting
(B) difficult
(C) strange
(D) humorous

3. In paragraph B, the word *irritating* probably means ______.

(A) new
(B) disorienting
(C) calming
(D) annoying

4. In paragraph D, the word *goals* means ______.

(A) points
(B) objectives
(C) customs
(D) ideas

5. In paragraph D, the word *rewarding* means ______.

(A) hopeless
(B) shocking
(C) exciting
(D) satisfying

SECTION III New Words Match the words on the left with their synonyms in the right column. *(4 points each)*

1. ______ colleague	a. end result
2. ______ despair	b. always, continually
3. ______ outcome	c. unbelievable
4. ______ inconceivable	d. opinion
5. ______ irrational	e. alert
6. ______ bias	f. receptive to new ideas
7. ______ open-minded	g. the beliefs and ways of life of a group of people
8. ______ culture	h. a feeling of being without hope
9. ______ aware	i. without reason or logic
10. ______ constantly	j. someone you work with

SECTION IV **Building Vocabulary** Add a negating prefix to the following words to change their meanings. *(2 points each)*

1. happy: ________
2. decisive: ________
3. aware: ________
4. honest: ________
5. accurate: ________

TOTAL ____ /100 pts.

Name ______________________ Date ______________ Score ______________

Frank W. Abagnale

SECTION I Reading Comprehension Read the passage. Then answer the questions that follow. *(5 points each)*

A Frank W. Abagnale has been affiliated with the FBI (Federal Bureau of Investigation) and is one of the world's most renowned authorities on money-related crimes. For over thirty years, he has acted as a consultant and has given numerous lectures on how to prevent money-related crimes to businesses and government agencies around the world.

B How did Abagnale become such an authority on these subjects? Strangely enough, he gained his keen insight into these topics by committing numerous money-related crimes himself. When he was 16, his parents got divorced. Shortly afterwards, he left home and went to New York on his own where he managed to get a job and open a bank account. Soon after, he committed his first crime, which involved writing bad checks against his own account. He made out several checks for more money than he had in his checking account. Because he knew that it was only a matter of time before his bank demanded that he pay the amount he owed, he opened new accounts at several other banks under different identities.

C As time went on, he came up with various clever ways to defraud banks. For example, he printed his own checks and convinced banks to cash them. He also took deposit slips from the bank, wrote his name on blank deposit slips and placed them back in the stack of blank ones, so when customers filled out deposit slips to deposit money into their accounts, the money went into his account instead of theirs. It is said that during a mere five year period, he managed to cash approximately 2.5 million dollars in forged checks. He supposedly cashed checks in every state in the United States and in 26 other countries!

D Eventually, Abagnale's luck ran out and he was arrested in France at the age of 21. He was sent to Perpignan's House of Arrest where he spent six months in squalid conditions and became very ill. Eventually, he ended up back in the United States to serve a 12-year prison sentence. However, halfway through his sentence he was released on the terms that he would use his "special talents" to assist the federal government and law enforcement agencies free of charge. He assisted these agencies by lecturing and teaching their employees how to prevent money-related crimes.

E Now over 30 years later, he is still associated with the FBI. In the meantime, he founded Abagnale & Associates, an organization that advises banks and various other businesses on fraud. He has written several popular books including *Catch Me If You Can*, which was made into a movie starring Leonardo DiCaprio and Tom Hanks. Frank W. Abagnale is now a multimillionaire from the money he has earned from his books and consulting business.

Sources: http://www.abagnale.com/aboutfrank.htm
http://en.wikipedia.org/wiki/Frank_Abagnale

1 What is the main idea of the reading passage?

(A) Frank W. Abagnale wrote fraudulent checks all over the world.

(B) Frank W. Abagnale has used his personal experience to help government agencies and businesses prevent fraud.

(C) Frank W. Abagnale has written several best-selling books, including *Catch Me If You Can.*

(D) Frank W. Abagnale was very good at defrauding people.

2 According to the reading, which of the choices describes something that Abagnale did NOT do in order to defraud banks?

(A) He printed his own checks and cashed them.

(B) He opened several accounts at different banks.

(C) He withdrew real money and photocopied it.

(D) He wrote his account number on deposit slips.

3 Abagnale cashed bad checks in how many countries outside the United States?

(A) 16

(B) 26

(C) 30

(D) 12

4 Why was Abagnale released from prison early?

(A) Because he had to serve another prison sentence in France.

(B) So he could write books and make movies about his crimes.

(C) Because he convinced authorities that he did not commit the crimes.

(D) So that he could help government and law enforcement agencies.

5 How long has Abagnale been assisting the FBI?

(A) over 30 years

(B) 12 years

(C) 26 years

(D) Since he was 16

SECTION II Strategies Use the context and your knowledge of word forms to choose the best meanings for the words in italics. *(5 points each)*

1 In paragraph A, *renowned* probably means ______.

(A) well-known
(B) intelligent
(C) wealthy
(D) helpful

2 In paragraph B, *keen* probably means ______.

(A) fast
(B) evil
(C) very good
(D) criminal

3 In paragraph C, *clever* probably means ______.

(A) inexpensive
(B) famous
(C) quick
(D) skillful

4 In paragraph C, *mere* probably means ______.

(A) long
(B) short
(C) difficult
(D) approximate

5 In paragraph D, *squalid* probably means ______.

(A) dangerous
(B) strange
(C) very dirty
(D) comfortable

SECTION III New Words Fill in the blanks with the correct word. *(4 points each)*

accessory	backslide	clean-cut	deliberated	responds
addled	burly	credits	draft	warily

1. Whenever the teacher asks a question, Seth does two things before he ________________. He thinks about his answer and he raises his hand.
2. Although Monique did not commit the crime, she was arrested for being an ________________ to the crime, because she let the thief stay in her home after the robbery and did not call the police.
3. Nobody could believe that Thomas was the murderer based on his ________________ appearance. He had short hair and no facial hair, and he dressed very conservatively.
4. The jury ________________ for three days before all twelve members agreed that the accused man was innocent.
5. Although she studied a lot for the test, she ________________ her tutor for teaching her some helpful ways of remembering new vocabulary words. Without her tutor, she might not have done as well on the exam.
6. Sue helped me ________________ an outline for my paper. Now I will be able to do the research and write a complete essay.
7. Once they are released from prison, many criminals ________________ because they are unable change their criminal tendencies and end up back in prison.
8. The fact that their car had been stolen ________________ their minds so much, that they were unable to fill out the police report properly.
9. The movie star was accompanied by three ________________ body guards, so nobody dared approach her for her autograph or to take photos.
10. When Carla heard the knock at her door, she opened it ________________ as it was late at night and she wasn't expecting anyone.

PART IV Building vocabulary Match the descriptive adverbs with their definitions. *(2 points each)*

1. ______ abruptly	a. directly
2. ______ nervously	b. fast
3. ______ personally	c. unexpectedly
4. ______ quickly	d. cautiously
5. ______ suspiciously	e. anxiously

TOTAL ______/100 pts.

Chapter 1 Test Answer Key

Section I

1. C **2.** D **3.** B **4.** A **5.** C

Section II

1. D **2.** B **3.** D **4.** B **5.** D

Section III

1. traditional **2.** channel **3.** slums **4.** finite
5. founder **6.** estimated **7.** reveal **8.** countryside
9. infrastructure **10.** sustain

Section IV

1. hand / shake **2.** over / crowded **3.** country / side
4. wild / life **5.** spring / time **6.** snow / field
7. hump / back **8.** big / horn **9.** tea / house
10. water / way

Chapter 2 Test Answer Key

Section I

1. C **2.** B **3.** C **4.** B **5.** D

Section II

1. A **2.** C **3.** C **4.** D **5.** C

Section III

1. vicious **2.** nondescript **3.** job **4.** revenues
5. V.P. **6.** global **7.** leading-edge **8.** low-end
9. ascend **10.** get the drift

Section IV

1. T **2.** T **3.** T **4.** T **5.** F
6. F **7.** T **8.** T **9.** F **10.** F

Chapter 3 Test Answer Key

Section I

1. C **2.** C **3.** A **4.** D **5.** A

Section II

1. B **2.** C **3.** A **4.** A **5.** D

Section III

1. e **2.** g **3.** a **4.** d **5.** j
6. i **7.** f **8.** c **9.** b **10.** h

Section IV

1. attribute **2.** deepen **3.** passing **4.** apparent
5. faction

Chapter 4 Test Answer Key

Section I

1. D **2.** A **3.** C **4.** C **5.** C

Section II

1. A **2.** A **3.** B **4.** B **5.** A

Section III

1. benefits **2.** communities **3.** compensation
4. virtually **5.** physical **6.** prevent **7.** affluent
8. found **9.** acquiring **10.** hence

Section IV

1. a **2.** d **3.** e **4.** c **5.** b

*Chapter 5 Test Answer Key

Section I

1. C **2.** A **3.** D **4.** B **5.** C

Section II

1. A **2.** B **3.** D **4.** C **5.** D

Section III

1. e **2.** g **3.** i **4.** d **5.** c
6. j **7.** h **8.** b **9.** a **10.** f

Section IV

1. handmade **2.** worn out **3.** machine-washable
4. well-read **5.** small-scale **6.** newlywed
7. timepiece **8.** home-based **9.** top hat
10. speedway

Chapter 6 Test Answer Key

Section I

1. B **2.** D **3.** C **4.** B **5.** D

Section II

1. A **2.** C **3.** B **4.** C **5.** D

Section III

1. enormous **2.** inclined **3.** convenience
4. mentality **5.** anticipated **6.** succulent
7. affordable **8.** amicable **9.** transform
10. specialties

Section IV

1. d **2.** c **3.** b **4.** e **5.** a

Chapter 7 Test Answer Key

Section I

1. C **2.** A **3.** B **4.** D **5.** A

Section II

1. C **2.** D **3.** D **4.** B **5.** A

Section III

1. influential **2.** suppress **3.** resigned **4.** compelling
5. founded **6.** commoners **7.** seized **8.** role
9. atone **10.** permeated

Section IV

1. drugstore **2.** unfinished **3.** reread **4.** outdoors
5. backyard **6.** defender **7.** overpriced **8.** decision
9. sportswear **10.** anti-war

Chapter 8 Test Answer Key

Section I

1. C **2.** B **3.** C **4.** A **5.** D

Section II

1. C **2.** B **3.** B **4.** A **5.** A

Section III

1. architect **2.** publish **3.** contemporary
4. on the lookout **5.** contraption **6.** in retrospect
7. mentor **8.** dud **9.** articulate **10.** assumptions

Section IV

1. c **2.** d **3.** a **4.** e **5.** b

Chapter 9 Test Answer Key

Section I

1. D **2.** B **3.** B **4.** A **5.** D

Section II

1. C **2.** A **3.** D **4.** B **5.** D

Section III

1. j **2.** h **3.** a **4.** c **5.** i
6. d **7.** f **8.** g **9.** e **10.** b

Section IV

1. unhappy **2.** indecisive **3.** unaware
4. dishonest **5.** inaccurate

Chapter 10 Test Answer Key

Section I

1. B **2.** C **3.** B **4.** D **5.** A

Section II

1. A **2.** C **3.** D **4.** B **5.** C

Section III

1. responds **2.** accessory **3.** clean-cut
4. deliberated **5.** credits **6.** draft
7. backslide **8.** addled **9.** burly **10.** warily

Section IV

1. c **2.** e **3.** a **4.** b **5.** d

Name ______________________ Date ______________ Score ______________

PLACEMENT **Test** **INTERACTIONS/MOSAIC** Reading

VOCABULARY I Choose the best word to complete each sentence. *(2 points each)*

Example Brazil and Argentina are the largest ______ in South America.

- (A) categories
- (B) cities
- (C) countries
- (D) neighborhoods

1. No one lives with Rosa in her apartment. She lives ______.
   - (A) alone
   - (B) lonely
   - (C) only
   - (D) together
2. Tom's family has 3 children, Amy's family has 3 children, Reina's family has 2 children, and Ben's family has 2 children. The ______ number of children in these families is 2.5.
   - (A) small
   - (B) average
   - (C) equal
   - (D) total
3. When teachers speak too softly and rapidly, it is ______ for their students to understand them.
   - (A) easy
   - (B) little
   - (C) different
   - (D) difficult
4. In many cultures, women do most of the ______. For example, they clean the floors and wash the clothes for their families.
   - (A) farming
   - (B) homework
   - (C) housework
   - (D) cooking
5. Mr. Lee's restaurant is successful because he always waits on his ______ politely and serves them wonderful meals.
   - (A) customs
   - (B) customers
   - (C) consumers
   - (D) users

6. In a basketball game, two teams _______ against each other to score points by throwing a ball into a basket.

(A) compete
(B) cooperate
(C) complete
(D) exercise

7. In this country doctors usually have high _______, or position in the society.

(A) profession
(B) situation
(C) state
(D) status

8. Many companies in the computer industry were started by very young people. For example, Bill Gates was only twenty years old when he and Paul Allen _______ the Microsoft Corporation in 1975.

(A) based
(B) discovered
(C) located
(D) founded

9. _______ up to 20% is customary in U.S. restaurants. Some places even add 15% to the bill for all parties of six or more.

(A) Waiting
(B) Tipping
(C) Buying
(D) Eating

10. I wouldn't go to the new mall just yet. If you can _______ another week or two, until the Grand Opening is over, the crowds will be much more manageable.

(A) hold out
(B) hold up
(C) wait on
(D) hold onto

VOCABULARY II Read each item and then answer the vocabulary question below it. *(2 points each)*

Example The city government recently announced plans to build a new road through Mountain Dale, a beautiful neighborhood on the south side of the city. The residents of Mountain Dale are angry about the road. Yesterday a group of them went to a meeting at City Hall to express their *views* on the city's plans.

Which of the following is closest in meaning to *views* as it is used above?

(A) pictures
(B) opinions
(C) sights
(D) beautiful scenery

1. The brain is divided into many parts. Each part serves specific and important functions. The cerebrum is the largest and most complex *area* of the brain. It controls thought, learning, and many other activities.

   Which of the following is closest in meaning to *area* as it is used above?

   (A) the size of a surface, calculated by multiplying the length by the width
   (B) a particular subject or group of related subjects
   (C) a particular part or section
   (D) a part of an activity or a thought

2. By studying the pyramids of Egypt, researchers have learned a great deal about ancient Egyptian *culture*. They have discovered, for example, that different social classes existed even in the earliest cities.

   Which of the following is closest in meaning to *culture* as it is used above?

   (A) activities that are related to art, music, and literature
   (B) a society that existed at a particular time in history
   (C) a scientific experiment of people from a particular country
   (D) education of people in a certain social group

3. Timothy is going to ride his bike around the world. In order to see all the countries and sights he wants to, before he begins his adventure, he will *map* his route.

   Which of the following is the closest in meaning to *map* as used above?

   (A) to pack bags for a trip
   (B) to plan the path of a trip
   (C) to prepare a bicycle for a trip
   (D) to talk about something

4. With today's computer networks, the *transmission* of data from one place in the world to another can happen instantly.

   Which of the following is closest in meaning to *transmission* as it is used above?

   (A) the process of working together on the same computer network
   (B) a job that involves traveling from one place to another
   (C) the set of parts of a vehicle that take power from the engine to the wheels
   (D) the process of sending information using electronic equipment

5. Roger has some annoying tendencies. For one thing, he's *inclined* to talk about himself and his achievements.

   Which of the following is closest in meaning to *inclined* as it is used above?

   (A) bending forward to say something
   (B) likely to do something or behave in a particular way
   (C) holding a particular opinion
   (D) talking a lot about the same thing

6. At medical centers throughout the United States, researchers are *conducting* investigations into the causes of heart disease.

Which of the following is closest in meaning to *conducting* as it is used above?

- (A) carrying out an activity or process in order to get information or prove facts
- (B) directing the playing of an orchestra, band, etc.
- (C) carrying something like electricity or heat to cure heart disease
- (D) guiding or leading someone somewhere

7. In recent years, it seems that headlines and articles about war and violence have *occupied* the front pages of newspapers everywhere.

Which of the following is closest in meaning to *occupied* as it is used above?

- (A) taken up time
- (B) lived in a place
- (C) controlled a place by military force
- (D) filled a particular amount of space

8. Studies in public schools have shown that *exposure* to art and music has many benefits for children. It improves their literacy, critical thinking, and math skills.

Which of the following is closest in meaning to *exposure* as it is used above?

- (A) a situation in which someone is not protected from risk or danger
- (B) attention that someone gets from newspapers, television, etc.
- (C) the chance to experience something
- (D) the act of showing something that is usually hidden

9. Ronald and James are roommates in a university dormitory. They have frequent arguments because Ronald prefers to go to sleep early and James always stays up late. Also, Ronald likes quiet while he studies, but James insists that loud music helps him concentrate. How can James and Ronald *resolve* these conflicts?

Which of the following is closest in meaning to *resolve* as it is used above?

- (A) make a definite decision to do something
- (B) solve again using new techniques
- (C) gradually change into something else
- (D) find a satisfactory way of dealing with a problem or difficulty

10. It is important that students learn to read and write before they go to college. In particular, they need to practice reading on their own and learn how to write a *succinct* and logical argument.

Which of the following is the closest in meaning to *succinct* as used above?

- (A) taking a long time to explain
- (B) correct
- (C) original
- (D) clearly and concisely expressed

Reading Section

DIRECTIONS: Read each passage and answer the questions below it. *(2 points each)*

Reading Passage 1

A How do you react to the taste of different foods, like coffee or lemon? Do they have a flavor that you like? Or do they taste very strong to you? Why do people react differently to different flavors?

B We all know that different people have different food preferences. Researchers have discovered some reasons for these differences. Your culture and your life experience are partly responsible for your preferences for certain foods. Your food preferences are also partly genetic. (Your genetic preferences are the ones that you were born with.) In order to discover people's genetic preferences, researchers use a chemical called PROP. People taste it and respond to the taste. To some people, PROP has no flavor. The researchers classify these people as "nontasters." To other people, the flavor of PROP is a little bitter, or sharp. These people are "tasters." Then there are the people who can't stand the flavor of PROP. They find it to be unbearably bitter. These people are the "supertasters." Tasters have more taste buds on their tongues than nontasters do, and supertasters have many more taste buds than tasters do. This explains why supertasters are more sensitive to PROP and to the flavors in certain foods. So if you think the flavors in coffee, grapefruit juice, and broccoli are very strong, you may be a "supertaster."

Example The topic of the reading passage is ______.

- (A) the flavor of coffee
- (B) becoming a supertaster
- (C) differences in people's taste sensitivity
- (D) research in the flavor of different foods

1. The main idea of the reading is that ______.

- (A) there are people who like different foods
- (B) there are cultural and genetic reasons for the differences in people's food preferences
- (C) some foods have a very strong flavor
- (D) PROPs can be used to identify different types of tastes

2. The meaning of *genetic* preferences is ______.

- (A) preferences for certain foods
- (B) preferences researchers have discovered
- (C) the preferences of some people
- (D) the preferences that people are born with

3. What is PROP?

- (A) a chemical
- (B) something that people are born with
- (C) a discovery
- (D) a researcher

4. Why do researchers use PROP?

(A) because it has no flavor

(B) to find out the responses to foods people were born with

(C) to discover the flavors in certain foods

(D) because people like its flavor

5. A food that is bitter has ______.

(A) no flavor

(B) little flavor

(C) a coffee flavor

(D) a sharp flavor

6. People who ______ are classified as *supertasters*.

(A) can't stand the flavor of PROP

(B) think that PROP has no flavor

(C) think that PROP tastes a little bitter

(D) like bitter flavors

7. Taste buds are probably ______.

(A) tiny pieces of food

(B) the small bumps on the surface of people's tongues

(C) chemicals in food that give it its flavor

(D) something in broccoli, grapefruit juice, and coffee

Reading Passage 2

A After a cold, snowy winter, many people look forward to the long hot days of summer. The normal heat of summer can be pleasant. However, it's important to be aware that excessive—that is, too much—heat can be dangerous. There are other summer weather dangers, for example, tornadoes, lightning, and floods, but excessive heat kills more people each year than any of these. According to meteorologists (weather scientists), a heat wave is a period of excessive heat that lasts two days or more. A heat wave stresses people and can cause illnesses. These illnesses include heat cramps, heat exhaustion, and heat stroke. The people who are at the greatest risk during heat waves are the elderly, babies, and those with serious diseases.

B High humidity (moisture in the air) can make the effects of heat even more harmful. As humidity increases, the air seems warmer than it actually is because it's more difficult for the body to cool itself through the evaporation of perspiration. During heat waves, meteorologists use the heat index to determine the level of danger. The heat index measures how hot it really feels when high humidity is added to the actual air temperature. As an example, if the air temperature is 95° F (Fahrenheit) and the humidity is 35%, the heat index is 98° F. But if the air temperature is 95° F and the humidity is 70%, the heat index is 124° F. Doctors say that even young, healthy people can die of heat stroke if they exercise outside when the heat index is high. During a heat wave, it's best to take it easy, drink plenty of water, and stay out of the heat as much as possible.

1. The main idea of Paragraph A is that ______.
   (A) people look forward to the long hot days of summer
   (B) too much heat can have dangerous effects
   (C) tornadoes, lightning, and floods are dangerous
   (D) meteorologists can define heat waves

2. The main idea of Paragraph B is that ______.
   (A) humidity is moisture in the air
   (B) meteorologists use the heat index during heat waves
   (C) high humidity increases the danger of high air temperatures
   (D) it's important to stay inside during a heat wave

3. The word *excessive* means ______.
   (A) too much
   (B) important
   (C) long
   (D) coming in waves

4. In the passage, lightning is mentioned as an example of ______.
   (A) excessive heat
   (B) a storm
   (C) a stress on people
   (D) a summer weather danger

5. A meteorologist is ______.
   (A) a doctor
   (B) a weather scientist
   (C) a space scientist
   (D) a dangerous weather condition

6. The heat index measures ______.
   (A) the amount of moisture in the air
   (B) air temperature
   (C) a person's body temperature
   (D) the temperature the body feels when heat and humidity are combined

7. Based on the information in the passage, which statement is true?
   (A) Young, healthy people are more likely to die from excessive heat than elderly people are.
   (B) The elderly, babies, and people with serious diseases are most likely to die from excessive heat, but it can kill young, healthy people, too.
   (C) Perspiration is a dangerous effect of excessive heat.
   (D) All heat waves include high humidity.

8. Why did the author write this passage?

(A) To warn people about the dangers of excessive heat and give suggestions about avoiding them.

(B) To give people useful information about the weather in the summer.

(C) To describe the work of meteorologists and their use of the heat index.

(D) To let people know how the body can cool itself naturally.

Reading Passage 3

A Even though education is compulsory (required by law) for children in the United States, it is not compulsory for them to go to a conventional school to get that education. In every one of the 50 states, it is legal for parents to educate their children at home, or to "home school" their children. Although no state requires parents to have special training to home school their children, the regulations parents must follow vary widely from state to state. New Jersey, for example, imposes virtually no requirements. In contrast, New York requires home schoolers to notify their school districts, file instructional plans and frequent reports, and submit the results of tests or other forms of assessment for each child.

B Increasing numbers of American families have been opting for home schooling. According to the National Center for Educational Statistics, about 1.1 million children were being home schooled in the spring of 2003. This represents an increase from the 850,000 who were being home schooled in the spring of 1999. In addition, the home-schooling rate—the percentage of the school-age population that was being home schooled—increased from 1.7 percent in 1999 to 2.2 percent in 2003.

C A survey conducted in 2003 asked parents to give their most important reasons for home schooling their children. Thirty-one percent cited concerns about the environment in conventional schools, including safety, drugs, or negative peer pressure. Thirty percent said that the most important reason was to provide religious or moral instruction. Sixteen percent said that the most important reason was dissatisfaction with academic instruction at conventional schools. Parents gave other reasons, too; for instance, many said that they wanted to strengthen family bonds or allow their children more freedom.

D It is difficult to show whether conventional schooling or home schooling works better. Home-schooled children tend to score significantly higher than the national average on college entrance tests. But educators say that it isn't easy to determine how meaningful the figures are, given the complexities of making direct comparisons. In the debate about home schooling, socialization is more of an issue than achievement. Advocates of conventional education believe that home-schooled children are at a disadvantage because they miss out on the kinds of social interaction and relationships with peers that are an essential part of a total education. Advocates of home schooling say that home-schooled children are not socially isolated; they think that home-schooled children have a larger social structure because they can be out in the world, in contact with people of different ages, and having experiences that they could never have in conventional schools.

DIRECTIONS: For each question, choose the best answer based on the reading passage.

1. The word *conventional* means ______.

(A) relating to a meeting

(B) following what is normal or usual

(C) following a religion

(D) educational

2. According to the passage, increasing numbers of American families are choosing home schooling. What information does the author give to support this statement?

(A) In every one of the 50 states, it is legal for parents to educate their children at home.

(B) Thirty-one percent of parents say that the most important reason for home schooling is concerns about the environment in conventional schools.

(C) The number of children who were being home schooled increased from 850,000 in 1999 to about 1.1 million in 2003.

(D) A survey was conducted in 2003.

3. Scan (look quickly through) the passage to find the answer to this question: How many of the parents surveyed in 2003 said that the most important reason for home schooling their children was dissatisfaction with academic instruction at conventional schools?

(A) 1.1 million

(B) 30 percent

(C) 16 percent

(D) 2.2 percent

4. Three of the following statements give facts, and one gives an opinion. Based on the reading passage, which one is the opinion?

(A) Home-schooled children are at a disadvantage because they miss out on some kinds of social interaction and relationships.

(B) Thirty percent of parents who home school their children said that the most important reason was to provide religious or moral instruction.

(C) The home-schooling rate increased from 1.7 percent in 1999 to 2.2 percent in 2003.

(D) The regulations that parents of home schoolers must follow vary widely from state to state.

5. Which paragraph gives information about the number of home-schooled children who attend college?

(A) Paragraph B

(B) Paragraph C

(C) Paragraph D

(D) That information is not given in the passage.

6. In Paragraph D, the author implies, but does not state directly, that ______.

(A) home-schooled children tend to score significantly higher than the national average on college entrance tests

(B) it should be easy to make direct comparisons between conventional and home schooling

(C) parents are not academically qualified to teach their children

(D) there is controversy about the benefits of home schooling

7. Based on Paragraph D, we can conclude that advocates of conventional education object to home schooling mainly because home-schooled children ______.

(A) cannot achieve academically

(B) cannot be compared to conventionally educated children

(C) are not well socialized

(D) have too much freedom

Reading Passage 4

A In recent years, the game of golf and golf tourism have grown in popularity in many places in the world. Golf, which traces its roots back to 15th century Scotland, is often viewed as a pleasant and harmless way to relax in a natural setting. But golf courses are not natural developments. They are artificial constructions that have a big environmental impact. As a result, there is often controversy about the building of golf courses.

B Opponents of the use of land for golf courses bring up a number of environmental concerns. One is that a golf course covers a great deal of land, typically up to 200 acres, and in the process of developing this land into a golf course, it is common for fragile native ecosystems such as wetlands, rainforests, or coastal dunes to be destroyed. Indigenous grasses, shrubs, and trees are removed and replaced by foreign vegetation. The construction process causes soil erosion and results in the loss of biodiversity and habitat for wildlife. Another concern is the amount of chemical pesticides, herbicides, and fertilizers used to maintain the grass on a golf course once it is established. These chemicals can result in toxic contamination of the air, the soil, the surface water, and the underground water, and this in turn leads to health problems for people who live near the course or downstream from it, for people who work at the course, and even for the golfers. Yet another concern is that golf courses require an enormous amount of water every day. Their water consumption can lead to depletion of scarce fresh water resources. These and other concerns about golf courses have provoked protests, most recently in east and southeast Asia, against planned golf projects.

C Designers, developers, and operators of golf courses have become increasingly aware of the environmental issues and of the protests. Consequently, they have sponsored research into more environmentally sensitive ways of constructing and maintaining courses. They believe that it is possible to build golf courses which protect and preserve the natural features of the landscape and natural habitats for wildlife. Their suggested practices include using native trees and shrubs, planting types of grass that require less water and are best adapted to the local climate, and using reclaimed water. Proponents of golf courses believe that these "green" golf courses can actually provide environmental benefits to their sites.

D However, even a "green" golf course is likely to result in some environmental degradation and loss of habitat. Therefore, many biologists and wildlife ecologists, such as Lawrence Woolbright, a professor at Siena College in Albany, New York, contend that the best places to construct new golf courses are places that are already degraded, such as former landfills (garbage dumps) and old industrial sites, rather than on undeveloped land. A golf course that transforms a degraded site into a scenic landscape with wetlands and woodlands and habitat for wildlife could actually be a benefit to the environment.

1. Which of the following is the best statement of the main idea of the reading passage?

   (A) Golf courses are artificial constructions, and are often built with no regard for the environment.

   (B) Controversies about golf courses affect the tourist trade.

   (C) Golf courses have significant effects on the environment, and these effects lead to controversy.

   (D) Golf and golf tourism are growing in popularity internationally, leading to a more negative effect on the environment.

2. What word is opposite in meaning to the word *indigenous*?

(A) native
(B) foreign
(C) natural
(D) vegetation

3. Which of the following is *not* mentioned in the passage as a negative environmental impact of a golf course?

(A) the destruction of fragile native ecosystems
(B) soil erosion caused by cutting down trees
(C) pollution caused by traffic and maintenance equipment
(D) depletion of scarce fresh water resources

4. Which of the following best summarizes the environmental concerns of opponents of the use of land for golf courses?

(A) They are concerned about the amount of land that a golf course covers.
(B) They are concerned about the impact of the process of constructing new golf courses.
(C) They are concerned about the impact of the maintenance of established golf courses.
(D) All of the above.

5. Based on Paragraphs C and D, we can infer that a "green" golf course is one that ______.

(A) consumes a great deal of water
(B) is environmentally sensitive
(C) is new and not degraded
(D) has grass, shrubs, and trees

6. Based on the information in Paragraph C, we can conclude that ______.

(A) it is certain that "green" golf courses have already been built
(B) it is certain that "green" golf courses will be built in the future
(C) it is not certain that any "green" golf courses have already been built or will be built in the future
(D) opponents of golf courses accept the idea that "green" golf courses can actually provide environmental benefits to their sites

7. Based on Paragraph D, we can infer that the author of the passage ______.

(A) agrees with Lawrence Woolbright
(B) disagrees with Lawrence Woolbright
(C) is willing to accept some environmental degradation and loss of habitat
(D) is opposed to all golf courses

8. What would be an appropriate title for this reading passage?

(A) A Brief History of Golf
(B) Golf's Dirty Side
(C) Why Make Golf Green?
(D) The Beauty of Golf

Interactions/Mosaic Reading Placement Test Answer Key

Vocabulary I

1. A **2.** B **3.** D **4.** C **5.** B
6. A **7.** D **8.** D **9.** B **10.** A

Vocabulary II

1. C **2.** B **3.** B **4.** D **5.** B
6. A **7.** D **8.** C **9.** D **10.** D

Reading Passage 1

1. B **2.** D **3.** A **4.** B **5.** D **6.** A **7.** B

Reading Passage 2

1. B **2.** C **3.** A **4.** D **5.** B **6.** D **7.** B **8.** B

Reading Passage 3

1. B **2.** C **3.** C **4.** A **5.** D **6.** D **7.** C

Reading Passage 4

1. C **2.** B **3.** C **4.** D **5.** B **6.** C **7.** A **8.** C

SCORING FOR INTERACTIONS/MOSAIC READING PLACEMENT TEST

Score	Placement
0–40	Interactions Access
41–55	Interactions 1
56–70	Interactions 2
71–85	Mosaic 1
86–100	Mosaic 2

This is a rough guide. Teachers should use their judgment in placing students and selecting texts.